WHEN I NEED

C000205247

WHEN I NEEDED
A NEIGHBOUR

Enabling Pastoral Care in the Local Church

PENNY NAIRNE

Marshall Pickering
An Imprint of HarperCollins*Publishers*

Marshall Pickering is an Imprint of
HarperCollins*Religious*
Part of HarperCollins*Publishers*
77–85 Fulham Palace Road, London W6 8JB

First published in Great Britain
in 1998 by HarperCollins*Religious*

A catalogue record for this book is
available from the British Library

ISBN 0 551 02976 5

Printed and bound in Great Britain by
Caledonian International Book Manufacturing Ltd, Glasgow

Scripture quotations are taken from the New Revised Standard Version Bible,
copyright © 1989, by the Division of Christian Education of the National Council of the
Churches of Christ in the USA and are used by permission. All rights reserved.

CONTENTS

FOREWORD

by Bishop John Taylor

There are some books on pastoral care which leave me cold. Either they are written in jargon of a particularly obscure and unintelligible kind, or they present the reader with a set of techniques of pastoral care which bear little relation to the realities which I have met with in my varied years of ministry.

It is to Penny Nairne's credit that she has avoided both these pitfalls. She is readable and easy to follow. She supplies page after page of real-life stories, some to illustrate her points, some to provoke discussion among her readers. There is nothing prescriptive here, except that she makes out the case for higher standards of mutual care in the life of the local church, with which no one will disagree. She does not belabour the clergy, for it is her contention that pastoral care is the laity's job. And she does not make the reader feel inadequate, as if locked out of a specialist circle of professional carers.

The atmosphere of this attractive book is sympathetic and encouraging, on the lines of 'you could try it this way'. The pastoral care it advocates and illustrates is love in action, prompted by the love of God in Christ but not throttlingly religious. It is tempered with sensitivity and is nothing if not practical. At the same time there is no hiding the author's conviction that pastoral care and evangelism are two sides of the one coin. Good pastoral care makes for effective evangelism, and evangelism without pastoral care is mere proselytism.

I congratulate Penny Nairne on this her first book. I hope it will not be her last.

John B Taylor

PREFACE

How do you respond when your neighbour tells you that his wife has cancer? What can you say to a young couple, who are excited about their wedding preparations, that may help them to build a secure marriage? How can you respond when someone starts pouring out a string of family problems, while you are waiting at the school gate and have to take your own tired child home? How, when there are already many pressures in your own life, can you stay alongside your neighbours in their sorrows and joys?

Lay people are inclined to believe that such questions belong to the clergy. But the Christian churches have for some time been moving away from the concept of the 'minister', 'pastor' or 'vicar' as the person who deals with all pastoral needs, presides at all the worship, preaches every sermon, undertakes all visiting, chairs every committee – to a fresh view, which is more in tune with the earliest practice of the church. Ordained ministers, while not relinquishing their own calling as leaders, are increasingly using their vocation and training to identify and enable the gifts of others.

I have been privileged to serve for the past twenty years as a lay minister on the staff of churches in three very different areas: suburban, urban and rural. I have had contact, as a tutor, with many people who have been studying 'Pastoral Care' as mature students and who have brought to their courses of study their wide and varied experience of life and of 'church'. I have talked to clergy and lay people in many parts of the country, about how they see 'pastoral care' and how they make it happen. I offer what I have learned, not claiming that this book is anything like a complete survey of the subject, but hoping that what I have written may be of use to those who are leaders – whether ordained or lay – in today's churches.

I have had in mind particularly those who need to develop the skills for a 'collaborative' style of ministry: discernment of gifts, encouragement and empowerment, training and equipping. The book aims to show, in particular, how neighbourly care can be made more effective – and no less sincere – through simple forms of organization and of training. It describes how fresh ideas are being put into practice by some local churches and it observes what has worked well, or less well. Section One considers the place of pastoral care today in the mission of the Church. Section Two sets out in a variety of contexts how people can be enabled to care more effectively. Section Three looks at specific methods and tools for training and discusses such difficult issues as confidentiality, authorization, 'boundaries' and motives.

This book does not set out to teach any specific caring skill. Rather it describes some of the ways by which a local church can empower all its members to care for each other and for the people around them – and so to become a truly caring community, nothing less than 'the body of Christ'.

Throughout the book I use the word 'minister' to denote an ordained member of the clergy, of any denomination. By adopting this usage, I do not intend to deny the belief, which underpins the book, that every Christian, whether ordained or lay, is called to 'ministry' – which is exercised whenever we are with other people, at home over the washing-up, in the workplace, in the train, on the bus, or in the check-out queue, as well as in the Sunday worship and mid-week groups of church life.

I am grateful to members of my family and many friends for their encouragement; to my husband, Patrick, for his patience and constructive criticism; to Vesper Hunter for her professional, shrewd, and always supportive comments; to my students at Westminster College and in the Oxford Diocese for their varied experience and ideas; to many people in many places who have given up their time to talk to me about what happens in their churches; and finally to Marlene Cohen, who suggested that I should write this book, for her guidance and friendship.

NOTES

- Bible quotations are from the New Revised Standard Version (NRSV) unless otherwise stated.
- This book contains many 'stories'. They are all based on real situations, although I have altered some details and used fictional names for all the places and people.

PASTORAL CARE
AND MISSION

CARING CHURCHES

'All who believed were together and had all things in common' ...
'The whole group ... were of one heart and soul' ... *'There was
not a needy person among them.'* (Acts 2:44; 4:32, 34)

'Unholy rows' ... *'church members split'* ... *'pensioner found dead
after days'* ... *'parishioners complain vicar never calls'* ... *'organist sacked'*. (Recent newspaper headlines)

Pastoral care today

Newspapers love to run sensational stories about the Church.
Such incidents suggest scenes that are very different from the
spirit of the earliest Christian communities. How attractive
some of the descriptions in the book of Acts make the early
church sound! But we know from St Paul's letters that these
communities were not always harmonious. The truth is that
most churches, now as then, have their successes and their failures, their good and bad times.

Is our church a 'caring community'?

All of us who have responsibility for exercising 'pastoral care' would like to think that our church – the one in which we exercise our own ministry – is a loving and united community, where people are cared for. We believe that Jesus's ministry, which was full of practical caring for people, should be our model. We are familiar with Jesus's teaching that happiness is found when we 'wash one another's feet' (John 13:14). But does this pastoral caring happen as fully and effectively as it could? How can those of us who have positions of leadership in the churches work with God to make it happen?

In this chapter we shall look at some different understandings of what is meant by 'pastoral care'. We shall consider whether there is anything unique about Christian care. We shall explore the calling of the Christian leader. Finally, by looking at New Testament descriptions of the earliest Christian groups, we shall find a vision to inspire our pastoral care today.

'Community care'

In Britain the term 'care' has in recent years acquired a specialized meaning in the context of the statutory social services. A 'carer' means a person who looks after an elderly or disabled person at home. 'Community care' usually refers to the statutory responsibility of the local authority to arrange a 'care plan' for everyone in need and to ensure that care of a high quality is provided for them.

There also exists a great deal of informal care provided voluntarily within the family or by neighbours and friends. This is the largest source of 'care'. Where it exists it is of immense value, but the reality is that it does not always happen now to the same extent as in the past. It is less common nowadays for family members to live near each other. There are no longer many villages or streets where everyone knows everyone else. Blocks of flats, detached houses on large estates, villages or suburbs that are largely deserted during the day: none of these lend themselves readily to the forming of 'caring networks'.

So even where professional care is well supplemented by neighbourly care, there are many gaps; and it is the very people who are most in need of friendship – because they are housebound, poor or shy – who can most easily be overlooked. So the 'enabling' of voluntary care includes the organizing of care, in unbureaucratic and sensitive ways, and the provision of training. It is helpful if the churches, other voluntary bodies and the statutory agencies, who all share the same goal, can work together in this enterprise.

Country connections

The word 'pastoral' derives from the Latin for a shepherd. Something of a rural tang still clings to it: for example, a bishop still carries a 'crook'. When we refer to a 'pastor', it is the shepherd image that we have at the back of our minds, however quaint that may seem among the traffic and tower blocks of the modern city. Since the drama of the Bible is played out against a largely rural backdrop it is not surprising that rural imagery is prominent – notably in the Psalms. So Jesus naturally made good use of 'pastoral' images: especially in his parables about shepherds (good and bad), sheep, sheepfolds, goats and wolves.

In a brief but vivid parable in Luke's Gospel, we are given a picture of one sheep out of a flock of a hundred wandering away and getting lost. We are shown how devotedly the shepherd cares for each one, will to go to any lengths to seek out the lost and will be jubilant when it is found (Luke 15:4, 5). In John's Gospel Jesus portrays himself as the 'good shepherd' who knows his sheep individually, devotes his whole life to them and is even willing to die for them (John 10:11).

The shepherd has continued to be a spiritually fertile image for Christians down the ages. Psalm 23 and the verses referred to above are among those texts that are universally familiar, either in their original form or in one of the many hymns derived from them. Paintings of the shepherd in his 'green pastures' and beside his 'still waters' were once popular for bedrooms, especially for children.

Nowadays, however, most people — in Britain at least — do not experience rural scenes as the backdrop for their everyday life. Does the image still have power, even for those who have never encountered a shepherd? Or is this picture less evocative than it once was? And perhaps less useful, since the shepherd is a solitary figure — and sheep are passive? The 'shepherd' picture has certainly played some part, down the centuries, in making the clergy feel that they must carry their burden of responsibility on their own, often feeling lonely in the task; and in turning the laity into a dependent flock, who accept — even cling to — their subordinate status. The individual shepherd going out to look for the one lost sheep, although reassuring as an image of God's care for each one of us, is not intended to convey any sense of shared responsibility.

Alternative images

Jesus used many pictures: the woman who loses one silver piece from a treasured necklace (Luke 5:8–10); the loving and patient father who welcomes back his feckless son (Luke 5:11–24); the parents who know how to give their children what is best for them (Matthew 7:9–11); the traveller who goes out of his way to help a stranger in desperate need (Luke 9:29–37); these images too have their limitations — but also their resonances for all time. Some other images for the one who 'cares' which may enrich our understanding of pastoral care have been suggested by contemporary writers. Sally McFague[1] puts forward 'mother', 'lover' and 'friend'. Alistair Campbell[2] suggests the 'wounded healer' and the 'wise fool'.

The 'wounded healer' is Christ, who is wounded indeed: betrayed and abandoned, mocked, tortured, crucified. But Christ is also able, through his very vulnerability, to heal: 'Through him God was pleased to reconcile to himself all things, whether on earth or in heaven, by making peace through the blood of his cross' (Colossians 1:20). Campbell maintains that this image is central to a proper understanding of pastoral care, which is offered not primarily 'out of our strength' but 'from our own experience of pain, fear and loss and our own release from their deadening grip.'[3] In practice, however, it is not always easy to see how we can best use our own woundedness to help someone else. It is patronizing – and usually a mistake – to say to another person: 'I know how you feel.' So what should we say ... what can we do ... in order to use our own experience helpfully? Practical suggestions are offered in the training courses described in Section Three.

The image of the 'wise fool' is drawn partly from St Paul's references to himself as 'a fool' and partly from the figure of the 'court jester'. We can indeed see much of 'the fool' in Jesus: in his challenges to conventional authority and received wisdom, his simple lifestyle, his refusal to take the way of worldly dominance, his questioning of the world's values. As Alistair Campbell writes: 'A caring which is pastoral must always seem a little bizarre, a little naive, and not a little irreverent, in the context of the values which our materialistic culture worships.'[4]

Campbell recognizes that the need for care to be given spontaneously and even 'foolishly' has to be balanced by the need to exercise discernment and skill and that 'such qualities rarely come naturally to us'. But on the other hand he seems anxious to emphasize the differences between professional care and pastoral care, and writes critically of attempts to develop counselling skills among lay people. He never quite faces up to the tension between the need for spontaneity and warmth and the need for knowledge and skill.

A group of people who were doing a 'Pastoral Care' course produced the following list of alternative images for the 'Christian carer': healer ... soldier ... servant ... teacher ... parent ... godparent ... partner ... spouse ... guru ... therapist ... midwife ... wise-owl ... 'lollipop' person ... security-guard ... guide-dog. Each of these images was found to have some value in highlighting a particular aspect of Christian pastoral care, but none of them could express it fully. For example, 'guide-dog' described an enabling relationship: the dog has been trained to use its gift of sight in order to enable its blind owner to live life to the full. This could be an apt image for a leader with a particular vision who wishes to use it to enable others. The limitation (which was quickly spotted by the students) is that whereas the dog can never give physical sight to the blind person, Christian leaders can and do enable others to 'see' – to grow into the same experience of life in Christ as they have themselves. Again, a 'spouse' is committed to sticking with you and looking after you; but this cannot be a fully satisfactory image for God's care for us, because human partnerships are secure only for a limited time, whereas God's commitment to his children never ends.

Every image, even the most biblical, has its strengths and limitations. We need, therefore, to work with a variety of images, if we are to gain any understanding of the breadth of God's care.

Does 'caring' come naturally?

The answer is: 'yes' and 'no'. On the one hand people have a natural desire to help their neighbours. Where a friendly network exists so that needs are known, people can often give enormous support just by being themselves and doing what their instincts suggest. On the other hand instinct can lead the most well-meaning people to make blunders: such as telling a bereaved person that they 'should have got over it by now' or a woman who has had a miscarriage that 'it was probably for the best'. Many other people have a natural diffidence, not wanting to 'interfere'. Or they may be prevented by embarrassment from giving the friendly greeting that a person in distress is longing for. Sometimes people are held back by judgements they make: 'That feckless young girl doesn't deserve any help!'

For all these reasons, 'neighbourliness' is no longer enough and even has some dangers. Natural friendliness, however, can be made more effective and people will be more confident in offering it, if they have acquired some understanding of human relationships and prepared themselves to meet a variety of situations. Church members need to be motivated to become more sensitive and effective in their everyday neighbourly relationships, through gaining a better understanding of how human relationships work. The result of this will not only be that more people will give and receive care, but also that more people will be given confidence in their own gifts and in using them to serve others.

- Suggestions for training – aimed at making neighbourly care more effective – are given in Section Three.

The place of pastoral care in the mission of the church

'The basic way to evangelise is through friendship. It's not through evangelists, or big meetings, it's through family and friends who humanise the Gospel: "if so-and-so is a Christian, it must be all right". We provide the bridge or the way for people to travel into the Christian faith' (Dr George Carey).[5]

In Jesus's own ministry 'care' and 'mission' went together. He made no distinction between care for the body and care for the spirit. He sent his disciples out to proclaim the Kingdom and to demonstrate the power of God's love by practising healing: 'As you go proclaim the good news, "The kingdom of heaven has come near." Cure the sick, raise the dead, cleanse the lepers, cast out demons' (Matthew 10:7, 8). The earliest communities of the New Testament church are described as caring for all the needs of their members, both physical and spiritual: and this 'caring' was done by those with the appropriate gifts, either to serve physical food or to serve 'the word' (Acts 6:3, 4).

Churches today similarly find that there is no clear distinction between 'pastoral care' and 'mission'. The one is the essential basis for the other. We cannot declare the Good News of God's accepting love unless we also demonstrate it in practice. When people really care for each other they want to share their joy in Christ. There is in the churches today an increasing recognition of the holistic nature of 'pastoral care' and of its central role in evangelism, together with many imaginative ways of putting this into practice.

- 'We have set up a number of "Good News Teams", which allow hesitant inquirers to come forward and join in events and activities in a non-threatening but Christian environment.'
- 'At a recent service celebrating the anniversary of the founding of a Christian housing association, the sermon pointed out that it was "quite impossible for the Church to concern itself only with 'spiritual' matters, for the spiritual was the very reason for the church's concern about the material and physical nature and well-being of God's children".'
- 'Mission is both service in the community and communicating the message of Christ's love and the need to respond to him.'[6]

The care offered by Christians should always be holistic in its approach: no single aspect of a person – their body, mind or spirit – can be cared for in isolation from the whole person. People must always be seen as 'brothers and sisters for whom Christ died', whose greatest need is for 'salvation'. It is signifi-cant that in Asia, particularly in Singapore, where Christianity is the fastest growing religion, pastoral care is seen as insepar-able from mission: 'Their evangelism is based in the parish and particularly home-based, weekday cell ministries combining evangelism and pastoral care.'[7]

'Effective evangelism will always involve social action and effective social action will always involve evangelism ... sharing the Gospel should not be kept separate from the relief of suffering.'[8] Any action we take, whether individually or corporately, which is aimed at people's welfare is in a real sense 'pastoral care', and all 'pastoral care' is in a real sense 'mission'. If we truly want the best for another person we shall long for them to know God, in all God's fullness – as Father and Lord, as Jesus Christ, saviour and friend, and as the life-transforming Holy Spirit, the powerful, invisible wind. 'Wanting the best' for a person in this sense is the underlying purpose of all our caring activities.

So much is clear. What is difficult is to know how to translate this longing in our hearts into practice in our day-to-day ministry – especially since, at a particular time, physical needs may be over-riding. When is it appropriate or helpful to speak of our own faith? If we are with someone who is perplexed or in pain, should we suggest praying together? Would it be helpful – or not – to raise questions about finding a purpose in life or about fears of death?

• These questions can be usefully explored within a training course such as that described in Chapter 11. Story No. 1 'Carol and Madeleine' could be used to stimulate discussion in a group.

'Maintenance' or outreach?

Canon Robert Warren, writing as the Church of England's National Officer for Evangelism, argues that the 'pastoral mode' of the Church is now outdated and needs to be superseded by the 'missionary mode'. 'The church in "pastoral mode" is a church in a Christendom setting where the vast majority of the population are baptised and, notionally at least, Christian ... The church in "mission mode" is, in contrast, set in a culture where a number of competing value systems ... exist alongside each other. Such is the present setting of the church.'⁹

Today, however, most churches are well aware that they are no longer operating in a 'Christendom setting'. This does not mean that a pastoral emphasis has become less important. On the contrary, as we have seen, pastoral activity remains at the heart of mission. It would be unfortunate if the word 'pastoral', with its biblical origins and honourable history, acquired a pejorative tone, implying that the pastoral activities of the Church are invariably introverted and irrelevant. Many churches, as well as caring for their own members, have initiated imaginative schemes to meet urgent needs in their communities – some of which we shall look at in Chapter Three. When, therefore, we are talking about the inward-looking condition from which we need to grow away, it is best to employ the term 'maintenance mode' (which is one that Canon Warren himself also uses), rather than 'pastoral mode', to describe it.

Being trapped in 'maintenance mode' is a danger for any local church. The Anglican parish clergy, for example, know that they are morally and legally responsible for maintaining the local parish church – its buildings, its public worship, its status and image, its finances. This responsibility weighs heavily upon them and can make it difficult for them to allow the church to move forward in faith. On the other hand it is sometimes the church treasurer or the members of the 'buildings committee' or of the 'fundraising group' who become obsessed with 'maintenance' of the status quo, with 'doing *this* and in *this* way because that's how we have *always* done it', and hostile to any suggestion that the church might engage with issues that are of real concern to the people around it.

When the congregation is getting fewer and older and everyone feels overstretched; when it is a struggle to pay its share towards central funds; when the church building or the organ needs expensive repairs again; when those who come for baptism or marriage appear to have no knowledge whatsoever of the very basics of the Christian faith; when simply to keep the church going is an exhausting struggle; then it will be hard indeed to 'let go' of the 'maintenance mode', and to make the bold decision to change into 'missionary mode'. Many traditional activities will have to be abandoned, but on no account must the 'neighbourly networks' — whether informal or more organized — be lost.

We will listen now to a few of the many Christians who are meeting these issues in their daily experience.

- Rachel, a woman in her fifties who belongs to her local church, sometimes helps her neighbour, Joanna, by taking her three young children off her hands for a few hours. In this way she is ministering to Joanna's body — her aching head and feet — but also to her spirit, her need for a bit of peace and time to herself. Rachel has another neighbour, Ellen, who is worried about her husband's drinking. Rachel and Ellen pray together regularly, which not only gives them both spiritual encouragement, but also helps Ellen to keep up her strength and maintain a positive outlook, so that she feels healthier in mind and body as well. Rachel finds that there are no separate compartments in her ministry.
- Amrik is a member of his church's pastoral team: 'I have recently been visiting someone who is seriously ill, who I knew had no religious faith of any kind. I longed to tell him about the Gospel — because it is so important in my own life. Lately I have had some conversations with him about the meaning of life and I have been able to tell him about the hope that Jesus brings. He seems interested and has started reading the Bible.' Amrik found that 'caring' led into 'mission' — even though that was not his conscious intention at the start.
- Frances is another lay person who exercises pastoral care in her church: 'I have learnt that one of the problems people face is judging themselves harshly and being self-condemning. I try to support them through including them in church activities and groups, so that they experience being acceptable

to God – without having to fulfil any set of criteria. I don't attempt to quote Scripture to people, rather I offer them companionship, showing them that I am like them and not perfect yet. I dare to hope that by seeing into my life they may choose Christ and begin LIFE!'

• Jackie Pullinger writes of her work among refugees in Hong Kong: 'Since being in the camp we have witnessed a change of atmosphere, the people are realizing that we are not there "just doing a job" but that we care for them. We will be setting up a bakery which will provide employment and training for some. We know that all we have to offer them is Jesus. He's their only hope and by genuinely caring for them we pray that they see Him ... we just love them and the rest is up to God.'[10]

The people in these examples have found that if they place every situation before God in prayer, and if they draw on their own experience, exercise sensitivity and sometimes have the courage to take a risk, then in practice the dividing lines between 'caring' and 'mission' disappear.

The calling to this holistic ministry is not for the clergy alone: occasions when lay people can give spiritual help by sharing their faith frequently occur. But they often occur unexpectedly and this is where training can help: by equipping people to use these opportunities to the full.

Christian care – is there any difference?

'Just as I have loved you, you also should love one another' (John 13:34). 'By this everyone will know that you are my disciples, if you have love for one another' (John 13:35).

The term 'pastoral care' is often used to distinguish care given officially by 'the church' from that delivered by secular agencies. The question arises: is there any difference? Christians are certainly not the only ones who can offer generous and effective care. But, as we have seen, Christian pastoral care is based on a wider understanding of what 'caring' means. It therefore has distinctive characteristics.

Motive: showing the love of God to everyone

As disciples of Jesus – committed to following his call, his teaching about God's love and his example – Christians want to make God's love real for every person. This is the prime motive for all the 'caring' activities of the churches. 'God actually loves me.' When this comes home to people, it makes all the difference to their self-confidence and esteem, so that – often for the first time – they believe they can do something with their lives. This realization of 'God's love for me' is often experienced initially through the loving help of neighbours – doing your shopping for you when you have flu, sitting with your aged relative when you need a break, listening and praying with you when you are on the brink of despair.

Quality: caring for the whole person

There is a special quality about the care offered in the name of Jesus, because it is not only 'caring for' people by meeting their immediate needs, but also 'caring about' their ultimate destiny as whole people – and is offered out of genuine love, which reflects the love of God. One writer suggests that the purpose of 'pastoral care' is 'to assist men and women ... to live as disciples of Jesus.'[11] Less overtly evangelistic and more warmly human is the following description: 'Pastoral care has one fundamental aim – to help people to know love, as something to be received and something to give.'[12]

Source of strength: drawing on God's power

Christians are strengthened and sustained in the work of caring by their confidence that God is with them and his power available to them. 'The immeasurable greatness of his power for us who believe' (Ephesians 1:19).

Everyone is involved and everyone benefits
If the Christian life is our response to God's love — shown to us supremely by Christ's life, death and resurrection — it follows that we are all called to use our gifts in being Christ to our neighbours. The practice of Jesus himself and of the earliest Christian groups suggest that in the church 'caring' should be carried out by everyone, not solely by the minister, priest, elders or 'pastoral team'. So in the life of a local church, pastoral care should be an activity shared by all: a reflection of God's love that we all offer to each other.

This caring always brings mutual benefits. 'A kindness rendered, praise given, understanding shown: these touch the lives of others and may change them. Certainly they change us.'[13] If you visit a person who is depressed, there are gains for both of you: you give the other person your companionship and your listening ear; you receive the satisfaction of being able to help. The other person's need is their gift to you.

Our vocation as Christian leaders

What, then, is our calling as ministers, pastors, leaders and teachers? We are to set an example of love in action, based on the model of Jesus himself. We are to show forth the love of God in the way we ourselves behave towards other people.

Here are some of the characteristics of God's love that we are called to demonstrate in our lives.

God loves each of us as precious individuals. Jesus said 'I know my own and my own know me' (John 10:14). Jesus healed people individually, even when they came out from among a huge crowd. Jesus spent time talking with individual people, even when they belonged to 'inferior' groups such as women or tax inspectors. Jesus called his disciples individually.

- So a good pastor knows each person individually and is not influenced by conventional stereotypes or predetermined judgements.

God is ready to nourish us with everything we need to grow into mature people. Jesus told Peter to 'feed my sheep' (John 21:17). The earliest Christians came together to hear reports of the wonderful things God had done and this was their nourishment: 'They called the church together and related all that God had done with them' (Acts 14: 27).

- So a good pastor nourishes people by offering them food for their minds and souls as well as their bodies and by giving them encouragement.

God leads us into the truth. Jesus promised that the Holy Spirit would 'teach' and 'remind you of all that I have said to you' (John 14:26).

- So a good pastor teaches people so that they understand better God's purposes in their lives.

God is ready to share the life of heaven with us. Jesus demonstrated in his own life his closeness to God his father and his need constantly to renew this closeness by spending time quietly with God. 'He went out to the mountain to pray; and he spent the night in prayer to God' (Luke 6:12). 'Abide in me, as I abide in you. Just as the branch cannot bear fruit by itself unless it abides in the vine, neither can you unless you abide in me' (John 15:4).

- So a good pastor helps people to find their own closeness to God, through their life in Christ.

God offers us 'abundant life' – life that is full and satisfying, that we can begin to find here and now. God works through people to bring this life to all people. God needs us to take responsibility, to be faithful, to work hard, to use all the gifts and resources we have been given as fully as possible. 'After they had appointed elders for them in each church, with prayer and fasting they entrusted them to the Lord in whom they had come to believe' (Acts 14:23). 'The apostles and the elders met together to consider this matter' (Acts 15:6).

- So a good pastor enjoys the work of ministry and the company of people; draws out the best in others; gives power to others; enables others to be themselves good pastors.

God is Trinity, therefore at the heart of God there is community. 'He will give you another Advocate, to be with you forever ... I will not leave you orphaned; I am coming to you ... You will know that I am in my Father, and you in me and I in you...' (John 14:16, 18, 20). Jesus lived and worked with his disciples in a close group. He never sent them out alone. Jesus attended the synagogue and the temple. He was often present at social occasions.

- So a good pastor shares life – its joys and its sorrows – with others, discovering how to live in community, how to build up 'the body'.

God is faithful. 'I will sing of your steadfast love, O Lord, forever ... I declare that ... your faithfulness is as firm as the heavens' (Psalm 89:1, 2). 'The one who calls you is faithful, and he will do this' (1 Thessalonians 5:24).

- So a good pastor does not let people down, by being ill-prepared for a meeting or an interview, double-booking, forgetting names, arriving late or failing to turn up. In both great and trivial matters the good pastor is efficient and well organized.

God loves us so much that he is even willing to be vulnerable and to die for us. 'I, when I am lifted up from the earth, will draw all peoples to myself ... he said this to indicate the kind of death he was to die' (John 12:32, 33).

- So a good pastor's whole life is lived in readiness to serve other people ... and in that service to be stretched and hurt – and even killed.

Past and present

The concept of 'every-member ministry' is rooted in the teaching and practice of Jesus and of St Paul. Jesus chose 'the twelve' – the group who were to be his special friends, close followers and future leaders – not from among those who had money or social position or university degrees or status in the synagogue. Instead he chose 'ordinary' people in his own neighbourhood – people who did practical jobs for a living – who were willing to give him their commitment. Jesus was able to discern what they were and what they might become.

Did they wonder at first why they had been chosen? Jesus showed them that in his Kingdom everyone would be able to serve, by using and developing their God-given talents. They had been called and would be valued for the way they used these gifts. Jesus himself was to be their pattern: 'You know that among the Gentiles those whom they recognize as their rulers lord it over them, and their great ones are tyrants over them. But it is not so among you; but whoever wishes to become great among you must be your servant, and whoever wishes to be first among you must be the slave of all. For the Son of Man came not to be served but to serve' (Mark 10:42–5).

The vivid accounts in the book of Acts of the earliest days after the resurrection remind us of the character of the first Christian groups: 'Now the whole group of those who believed

were of one heart and soul ... With great power the apostles
gave their testimony to the resurrection of the Lord Jesus, and
great grace was upon them all. There was not a needy person
among them...' (Acts 4:32–4).

St Paul had much to say to the churches about 'the body':
'If we live by the truth and in love, we shall grow completely
into Christ, who is the head, by whom the whole Body is fitted
and joined together...' (Ephesians 4:15, 16 Jerusalem Bible). He
also said: '...we, who are many, are one body in Christ...'
(Romans 12:5).

The 'body' – the community – was made up of people with
varied talents making widely varied contributions to the whole.
In his letters St Paul helped the early Christian communities to
work out what his teaching meant in their day-to-day life
together.

Down the centuries there have been many departures from
this early vision and practice. Confusion has often developed
between 'gifts', 'role' and 'status'. At the time of the Reforma-
tion there was an urgent need to bring the Church back to the
Gospel understanding of ministry, with its emphasis on 'calling',
commitment and faith. Luther taught that 'good works' contributed nothing to salvation: that we are saved only by faith.
This meant that 'priests' or 'ministers' were simply carrying
out the service to which their faith directed them and for which
they were equipped – and they were thus on a level with everyone else.

By the nineteenth century there had developed in Britain a
high degree of dependence by the laity, for both teaching and
pastoral care, on the ordained clergy. Today many church members still assume that this is the right and proper relationship
between 'minister' and 'people'. But today the churches are
being recalled to the true situation: all are 'laity', all are 'ministers', all are 'priests' – with Jesus himself as our only 'high
priest' and the ordained clergy as servants of all.

The importance of this shift has been matched, over the last
century and a half, by a growing sense of the need to care for

the unfortunate. Many projects for voluntary provision have been developed, which have often been inspired by the consciences of lay Christian people. During the twentieth century much of the responsibility for care has been gradually taken over by 'the welfare state', but now the pendulum is swinging back again, partly as a reaction against what is seen as a 'dependency culture'. State benefits are being reduced, and some of the provision of care is being handed over to private businesses.

We are seeing a change in the balance between the roles of the state and of the voluntary organizations. Although for many the standard of living is higher than ever before, there is also widespread poverty: beggars on our streets, whole families living in one scantily furnished room, mothers going without food themselves in order to feed their children, old people dying unnoticed, young men being drawn into drug taking and crime because they have no jobs and no sense of purpose in life. In the face of all this deprivation, there is a renewed need today for voluntary provision and a growing recognition that the churches and other religious groups – together with a great number of other voluntary organizations – are well equipped to initiate many kinds of caring and enabling activity.

Collaborative ministry

Improved education for everyone (and particularly for women), means that a wider spread of people are able and willing to take responsibility and exercise leadership. So all the churches are now giving more attention to collaborative patterns of ministry, in order to make better use of the talents of all. The Principal of a theological college makes a point of reminding ordinands that 'we are all laity' and that this understanding should lead them to exercise a shared ministry. There is an increase in the numbers of non-stipendiary ministers who work in lay occupations. They expect to work with others in a team.

Differing gifts

In the earliest Christian groups there were apparently no rotas or timetables arranging who did what, no 'job descriptions': people simply contributed whatever they could. But as the churches grew, some degree of organization became necessary. The practice developed of appointing people to do jobs suited to their particular abilities.

> Now during those days, when the disciples were increasing in number, the Hellenists complained against the Hebrews because their widows were being neglected in the daily distribution of food. And the twelve called together the whole community of the disciples and said, 'It is not right that we should neglect the word of God in order to wait on tables. Therefore, friends, select from among yourselves seven men of good standing, full of the Spirit and of wisdom, whom we may appoint to this task, while we, for our part, will devote ourselves to prayer and to serving the word.' What they said pleased the whole community, and they chose Stephen, a man full of faith and the Holy Spirit, together with Philip, Procurus, Nicanor, Timon, Parmenas, and Nicolas, a slave of Antioch. They had these men stand before the apostles, who prayed and laid their hands on them. (Acts 6:1–6)

There are several points to notice in the above account of the growing community:

• Care for people had to be organized
• People were enabled to use and develop their particular gifts
• They worked together – collaboratively
• Everyone concerned was carefully consulted
• They continually prayed for God's guidance and blessing.

Organize, enable, collaborate, consult, pray

If we keep these points in mind they will help us to hold a biblical vision of pastoral care before us; to consider constructively some of the difficult issues that arise; to identify the principles of 'best practice' and to work out practical plans for enabling pastoral care in our own local situation.

Story for discussion

1. Carol and Madeleine

TOPICS
* Caring for the whole person
* Sharing our faith
* The need for training
* Discerning when professional help is needed
* How much time should I give?
* Letting go

This story illustrates how natural and easy 'caring' can be, how it can also become demanding and difficult and how simple training can give people extra skills and the right touch in sharing faith.

Carol is a young mother with a toddler and a new baby, living in a small town. Her husband left her a few months ago. The baby was born prematurely and had to remain in intensive care for several weeks. When she came home he was still very small and needing constant feeds. A group of Carol's friends in the town felt concerned about her and decided to do something practical to help. So they formed a rota to cook and deliver to her a good hot evening meal every day, because they guessed she would never have time to cook for herself and it was important for her to keep up her strength. The scheme was a success, but after a while it became obvious that Carol was lonely and needed friends. She would be reluctant to let the meal-deliverer go, because she was desperate to talk about her problems. So her friends found that the time commitment was increasing and, more seriously, that they were becoming unofficial 'counsellors' and did not feel adequate for this role.

First discussion

1   What was to be done? Should Carol's friends withdraw
    their help, not wanting to get too involved?
2   Should they just go on doing their best to meet her needs,
    'playing it by ear'?
3   Could they find some guidance to help them?
4   Should one of them discuss the situation with Carol,
    suggesting, for example that she might need professional
    help?

One of these friends, Madeleine, mentioned that a course entitled 'Listening and Caring', put on by the local churches, was just starting. Several of Carol's friends decided to join. They experienced some 'listening exercises', to help them to develop better 'listening skills'. [This course is described in Chapter 11.] They then saw that professional counselling was not needed and they themselves could listen to Carol in a constructive way, helping her to find her own path through her problems.

Madeleine felt that, in addition to practical help, Carol needed a faith and a purpose for her life and longed to help her to get to know Jesus Christ. Madeleine had been learning recently about how to share faith appropriately and soon found she could talk with Carol at this deeper level.

Second discussion

Did Madeleine choose the right time and the right way to share her faith with Carol?

CARING PEOPLE

'When Jesus heard this [the death of John the Baptist], he withdrew from there in a boat to a deserted place by himself. But when the crowds heard it, they followed him on foot from the towns. When he went ashore, he saw a great crowd; and he had compassion for them and cured their sick.' (Matthew 14:13, 14)

'We rejoice when we are weak and you are strong. This is what we pray for, that you may become perfect.' (2 Corinthians 13:9)

'The Gospel is wider than just the people who are in church. It's about everyone in the community.' (A minister describing the role of the church in an inner-city estate)[1]

Good works — study and action

Nowadays we make 'Pastoral Care' a subject for study — prominent in the syllabus at theological colleges and for mature students doing 'distance learning' courses. Many helpful books have been written on this subject and more appear every month.

Pastoral care is also prominent today on the practical programme of the churches. A variety of ministers and lay members of local churches were asked how they see 'pastoral care'
and how they carry it out:

'After two years of prayer and planning we have just
started a "Church Neighbours" scheme.'

'I regard the PCC as almost like an "eldership": the members lead teams for pastoring and outreach.'

'Our home groups are the basic unit for pastoral care.'

'In our group of rural churches it's impossible for one person to do all the pastoral visiting, so each village now has a
small team with a trained leader.'

'If anyone comes into our church upset, they will not go
away without somebody comforting them. Caring is not
overdone, but it is prominent.'

'We have set up an ecumenical "Care Group", which
arranges baptismal follow-up and welcoming of newcomers to the area. Last Christmas we delivered bowls of
hyacinth bulbs to people who live alone and we are now
considering giving out cards at funerals, offering comfort,
friendship and a listening ear to those who might be in need
of support.'

'After the service last Sunday two women met each other
and discovered that they had been living a few doors apart
for the last three years.'

'We are planning a "Community Weekend", with a fair
in the morning, a garden-party in the afternoon, dancing
in the evening, and a service in the morning. Another

weekend we are organising a hike. People are getting excited about doing things together.'

'I suggested holding a service for all the "good neighbours" in our area and nominations came flooding in. People have stopped to think what others do for them, and people have felt appreciated.'

'Pastoral care' is increasingly understood as a central aspect of the life of any Christian community. It is seen today not as something that one person does *to* or *for* another, but as a natural growth of *mutual* support within a loving community: 'Mrs Green does old Mr White's shopping and calls in for a chat when she delivers it – week in, week out.' The loving practical help given by individuals to individuals – this is what most of us think of as the essence of 'caring'. But the truth is that every human activity has a caring aspect. In the workplace or in the kitchen, everything we do can be done in ways that either ignore, or take account of, the sensibilities of people. 'Pastoral care' by the church may suggest visits to people who are housebound or in hospital, a listening ear for the anxious, prayer with the sick, comfort for the bereaved. But this is not the whole scope of caring by the church. Every activity generated by a local church – joining in worship or in social events, being a sidesperson, writing for or editing the church magazine, organizing the cleaning rota, looking after money, designing posters, tending the church grounds or belonging to a home group – all these can be done in a caring spirit and with an eye to what will build up and nurture people.

All church activities bear upon the welfare, in the fullest sense, of people: and therefore involve pastoral care. Most churches have an understanding of pastoral care that goes even wider than these internal activities: they find that 'caring', to be effective, often needs to be carried out through organizing projects that involve many people. So pastoral care can be all of the following – and this list does not claim to be complete:

- Visiting those who are housebound or ill, at home or in hospital.
- Neighbours looking out for each other's needs.
- Setting up a 'road warden' or 'fish' scheme (housebound or sick people have a card with a fish on it which they put in their front window if they need help; neighbours who see the fish go in and offer help).
- Praying for people in all kinds of need: during corporate worship, in groups or individually.
- Helping people to grow in prayer.
- Providing 'quiet times': quiet days and retreats.
- Encouraging people to read the Bible.
- Introducing people to a range of Christian books.
- Making sure that the church's public worship is welcoming and accessible to all – including those who cannot read or do not belong to a 'book culture'.
- Following up the opportunities of continuing contact when people approach the church for a baptism, wedding or funeral.
- Providing opportunities for people to learn:
  – basic doctrine, so that they really know about their faith;
  – how to listen well, to give them confidence to be 'good neighbours';
  – about ethical issues, such as how money and possessions should be viewed.
- Setting up 'housegroups', where people have a sense of belonging, of being known and of being able to trust each other.
- Giving people support in their weekday life, including their jobs – if they are employed.
- Helping church members to talk about their faith to those who do not know Jesus Christ.
- Seeing that the church is efficiently managed, so that people's questions and needs are attended to promptly.
- Setting up and running community projects (such as resource centres, holiday clubs, furniture stores, credit unions).

- Using church buildings in ways that benefit the whole community.
- Putting pressure on those responsible for the statutory services to improve 'community care' locally.
- Working politically to change the way society is organized.
- Helping people with their financial problems, including debt.
- Responding to a sudden local disaster.
- Giving support to people who have been bereaved – or suffered other kinds of loss.
- Dealing with 'callers' humanely and wisely.
- Relating sensitively to people with unconventional lifestyles.
- Giving support to people in all kinds of 'relationship' problems.
- Communicating well, so that people know what is going on and feel they belong.
- Preparing couples for marriage and giving them support in marriage.
- Encouraging and helping parents.
- Developing a healing ministry.
- Helping people to find individual spiritual companionship and guidance, through a 'spiritual director' or 'soul friend'.
- Knowing about other sources of help to suggest.
- Accepting that the best support is often simply to be there, to stay alongside.

In the chapters that follow we shall look in more detail at some of the above activities. We shall look, in particular, at the best methods of encouraging, setting up and sustaining these caring activities, together with practical ways through which good pastoral care can be developed. We shall consider how the people involved can be helped to become more skilful, confident and sensitive.

In this chapter we shall look at some issues that confront a local church as a community, when it is considering – or reviewing – its active involvement in pastoral care. They are also of concern to individual church members.

- Should we concentrate on individual care or on social action?
- Who is cared for? Only 'members' or everyone? How are people referred for help?
- Who does the 'caring'? What is the role of the ordained 'minister'? Is visiting by the clergy important?
- Is 'authorization' or 'accreditation' needed by those who 'care' in the name of the church?
- Should we put limits on our caring? What boundaries should we set?
- How can we give support to those whose moral principles differ from our own?

Individual care or social action?

'We share responsibility not just for individual souls but for tackling corporate sin and pointing to the spiritual goals of society as a whole.' (Statement on political action by the House of Bishops)[2]

'So-called "church life", however seductive and comforting, must never become a substitute for the Christian struggle "to build Jerusalem in England's green and pleasant land".' (Bishop Michael Marshall)[3]

'In the East End I learnt that you also had to talk about structures and the lack of opportunities open to people. If you wanted to love your neighbour you couldn't just do something for the individual … You had to ask questions that might make you unpopular at the town hall.' (Bishop David Sheppard)[4]

'The current public debate about morality should not cherry-pick aspects of morality to do with personal behaviour but should encompass the ordering of society and tackling the deep spiritual wounds of social exclusion.' (Dr Andrew Purkiss, reporting the views of Dr Carey)[5]

Many individual Christians feel called to take an active role in national or local politics. They want to improve 'the ordering of society' by tackling 'corporate sin' and by asking the questions 'that might make you unpopular at the town hall'. They believe, with General de Gaulle, that 'politics are too serious a matter to be left to the politicians.'[6]

When, however, the members of a local church want to heal 'the deep spiritual wounds of social exclusion', they usually prefer to become involved in practical projects which are of immediate value to the people in their own area. Many of the volunteers on whom local community projects — such as 'meals-on-wheels', day centres, luncheon clubs, hospital driving, night shelters, resource centres — depend are church members. In some places this involvement of individuals may well be the best expression of the church's commitment to community issues.

None the less, where the circumstances in which people live prevent even their most basic needs — for food, shelter, a job, security, affection — from being adequately met, then the only hope of making effective care available to them may lie in a group of people deciding to take action together. Angela Sarkis, Chief Executive of the Church Urban Fund, shares this view: 'A church leader who had been involved in working for five years in a CUF-supported project in London felt that by engaging in the real welfare issues affecting local people, the local church had gained credibility in its task of sharing the Gospel. People described the church as "the church that helps the unemployed" — and a number of them had come to find faith.'[7]

Ministers and members of a local church or group of churches become aware of a particular need. Someone has a vision for what could be done. A decision is made — ideally in co-operation with local statutory bodies — to initiate a community project. Enthusiasm is generated. Money is raised. Premises are found. An idea which at first may have seemed impossibly ambitious becomes a reality. The church is seen as 'the church that helps'.

In Chapter 3 we shall return to this subject and look more closely at some of the widely different community projects initiated and run by local churches.

Who is to be cared for? Only members or everyone?

When informal neighbourly networks are in play no distinctions are made between members of the church and non-members: you go to the help of your neighbours simply because they are your neighbours. But when we look at the more organized activities of local churches, do we see the responsibility for pastoral care being restricted to 'church members' or is it extended to everyone?

In the Church of England ministers have a formal duty to look after every person who lives in the parish. In practice, and especially in densely populated urban areas, such coverage is impossible. And in an area where Christian churches of other denominations are active (as well as other faith groups), it would also be inappropriate. Anglican clergy respond as best they can to requests for help and to a greater or lesser extent share their responsibility with lay people.

In an Anglican parish it is in any case not clear who is – or is not – a 'member' of the church. There is a formal 'electoral roll' and sometimes an informal 'family roll' is also kept. In spite of these, 'membership' tends to be undefined and fluid. In the free churches membership is clearer: therefore pastoral care for members can be assured. But the expression of Christian love can never be restricted and most churches see it as part of their calling to try to meet the needs of a wider range of people than those who have formal church membership.

Needs cannot, however, be met if they are not known. For this purpose some churches find it useful to carry out an audit or survey of their area. In most places doctors, community nurses, health visitors and those who organize meals-on-wheels or day centres will refer people who need help. Ministers often keep lists in well-thumbed notebooks or card indexes – or they may simply rely on keeping names in their heads. But if the minister has a sudden heart attack and dies, all those details about Mrs Jones's children or Frank's and Fred's long-standing feud will be lost. It is better for names and discreetly worded information to be kept on a computer database. (If it holds any more information about people than names and addresses it must be registered under the rules for Data Protection.)

A certain degree of efficiency in passing on information and keeping records helps to ensure that pastoral care is available when it is needed and in the way it is needed. Efficient arrangements ensure that neighbours have confidence that it is worth taking the trouble to pass on information to the appropriate person – usually either to a minister or to the organizer of the pastoral team – when they know someone is in need of help that they cannot give themselves.

Who does the 'caring'? What is the role of the ordained 'minister'? Is visiting by the clergy important?

'Follow me,' said Jesus to the fishermen, Simon and Andrew, 'and I will make you fish for people.' After his resurrection he told Simon to 'feed my sheep' (Matthew 4:19; John 21:17).

All ministers regard pastoral care as an important part of their role. They are generally expected to be endowed with pastoral gifts – but in reality they are not all equally talented in this respect. In the case of some ministers, pastoral care would be improved if, while accepting their own ultimate responsibility for ensuring that people were cared for, they did not think they had to do it all themselves. Some ministers would be wiser to concentrate on teaching, while arranging for most of the pastoral care to be taken on by others. Some lay church members have a special sense of being called to a caring ministry. They may also have particular gifts – of personal warmth and sensitivity, for example – which, if recognized, can be put to good use.

Lay people in general expect the church to care for people and by 'the church' they usually mean the clergy. In the past, ministers were often judged by their 'flock' according to the amount of 'visiting' they managed to do. And the clergy felt they had a duty to give high priority to this. The visits were not usually aimed at 'pastoral care' in any deep sense, but were simply meant to make personal contact with as many parishioners or church members as possible. The minister in one small country town thinks this is still important today. He visits intensively for four weeks each autumn, reckoning to knock on the door of every house. But more often the scene has changed in ways that make such 'blanket coverage' by clergy impossible: reduced numbers, financial constraints, altered lifestyles – fewer people at home by day, the television on all evening.

Is 'authorization' or 'accreditation' needed by those who 'care' in the name of the church?

This question is difficult to answer conclusively. In many dioceses or districts official recognition in some form is available. In several Anglican dioceses there have for many years existed schemes for the authorizing of lay people, who have taken some practical training, to work in parishes as 'Pastoral Assistants'. These schemes ensure that help reaches those in distress – and that those who offer help have been trained at least to know what they should *not* do! 'Official' endorsement gives confidence to both those offering pastoral care and those needing care. Irene was recently appointed to the voluntary role of administrator for a group of churches: 'It is helpful that I am known throughout the area, but even so I would have valued some kind of commissioning at the time when I took up the job. It would have helped me to co-operate with the churches as I developed the work.'

On the other hand, the existence of 'accreditation' may make those who exercise other kinds of ministry, such as doing the flowers, making coffee or acting as 'welcomer', feel *less* confident. In one Anglican diocese a decision was made a few years ago not to proceed with any scheme for the accrediting of pastoral assistants. It was feared that people might be put off from offering to help with anything unless they had done a course or received a certificate.

Lay people are, however, asking for training and authorization in order to exercise pastoral care in the name of the church. In response to such requests some local churches have decided to set up their own schemes.

Should we put limits on our caring?
What boundaries should we set?

'When I am listening to someone, I get so caught up in their problems I cannot think straight ... I go home exhausted from their pain. And then I worry about them all night and the next day. I have worries enough of my own. I don't think I can do this sort of work with people. It is too hard on me.'[8]

'How can I bear the heavy burden of your disputes all by myself?' (Deuteronomy 1:12).

Countless examples could be quoted of care being given unstintingly and without limits. A Methodist writes of her church in Sheffield, 'There is one old church member with a degenerative illness whose husband cared for her full-time until his sudden death. For several years now she has been enabled to go on living in her own home by a team of people who supplement what her family is able to do. Very little is ever said about this, but it goes on happening quietly year after year.'

People sometimes rush to help, however, and then find that they and their families are drawn in far beyond what they expected and against the best interests, in the long run, of the other person. Whereas a professional counsellor can confine a client's outpourings within a one-hour appointment, the caring neighbour may have difficulty in setting any boundaries – and may get exhausted and even resentful.

• These issues are explored in the basic training course described in Chapter 11 and in Handout 4 in Chapter 12. Story No. 2 'Tracy, Mandy, Martha and Jack', given at the end of this chapter, could be used for discussion.

Our principles

How can we listen to and support someone who holds different ethical principles from our own – or whose way of life flies in the face of the standards of behaviour we ourselves try to follow? Counselling theory tells us: 'If we are to be effective, we must suspend our own judgments for a while in order to get the other person into accurate focus.'⁹ Does this mean that we are to dismiss our strongly held personal moral principles as mere prejudices, which we ought to do our best to put on one side when we are caring for another person? This can be a particularly acute dilemma for a minister, but can also be a problem for lay Christians when they encounter people who need their help but whose values are different from their own.

There are three biblical models that can help us here.

First, 'Love the sinner, but hate the sin.' This was Saint Augustine's summary of Jesus's practice, when he met a woman taken in adultery. 'Let anyone among you who is without sin be the first to throw a stone at her ... Where are they? Has no one condemned you? ... Neither do I condemn you. Go your way, and from now on do not sin again' (John 8:7, 10, 11). Jesus showed compassion for the woman and gave her practical help by rescuing her from the terrible punishment of being stoned to death – but he also told her not to repeat the sin she had committed.

There is nothing kind or helpful in concealing our own principles from another person. If we truly 'care about' them we cannot wish them to continue along a path that we believe is separating them from God. But we need to be clear — and to show, in our words and attitudes — that our principles are our own and that we are not imposing them on anyone else. Bishop Hugh Montefiore is clear that 'pastoral care involves the application of moral principles to the lives of individuals', but that this must be done 'with sensitivity, firmness and compassion'.[10]

Second, people cannot be lumped together in general categories and given labels: the poor, the disabled, the wicked. Jesus did not give lectures on ethical theory in general. Rather he had many encounters with individuals, which became 'learning experiences' for those people and their friends — and for his disciples. When Jesus taught in words he usually did so by means of stories about individual people. As pastors we always have to deal with — to 'care about' and to 'care for' — a particular individual person, who is in a particular situation here and now.

Third, we must never forget that we are sinners ourselves, that we too constantly fall short of even our own most passionately held principles. None of us is in a position to make judgements, none of us can 'cast the first stone'. 'Somehow the minister must let the person know that, in a fundamental sense, he is "in the same boat"; he too is under judgment and in need of grace.'[11] When we want to help someone else it is important to keep this in the forefront of our minds. We are less likely to exert any influence if we seem to be setting ourselves up as 'holier than thou'.

At the same time, our own *example* certainly influences other people and speaks louder than anything we *say*. 'Not everyone who says to me "Lord, Lord", will enter the kingdom of heaven,' said Jesus, 'but only the one who does the will of my Father in heaven' (Matthew 7:21). The Letter of James declares 'If any think they are religious, and do not bridle their tongues but deceive their hearts, their religion is worthless. Religion that is pure and undefiled is this: to care for ophans and widows in their distress and to keep oneself unstained from the world' (James 1:26, 27). We may never know what effect we have had

on another person, but experience suggests that what we *are* —
which includes the ideals we struggle towards — often has a
more powerful influence than we realize.

Our prejudices

How can we recognize our prejudices? This is difficult, because to
a large extent they are built into us through our upbringing and
our surroundings. They are often, however, strengthened by the
limitations imposed by language. For example, it is now widely
accepted that we should avoid referring to groups of people as
'*the* handicapped' or '*the* poor', but to refer instead to 'handicapped people' or 'poor people'. This is important, because in
talking about 'the handicapped', we distance this group of people
from us. And we overemphasize their group identity at the
expense of their individuality as separate people, each with a distinct personality and distinct needs. We lump them together and
give them all the same label, a label which reflects our own preconceived image of just one aspect of their situation.

A 'national forum on values' was set up by the Schools Cur-
riculum and Assessment Authority in 1996. It was reported that
some members were concerned about a particular aspect of the
evidence they received from schools which stated that their aim
was to 'respect or tolerate everyone' when in fact 'they did not
tolerate bullies or racists'.[12] The suggestion here is that some
youngsters could be labelled as 'racists' or 'bullies' and should
then be deprived of 'respect' or 'tolerance'. So neither Augustine's precept that we should love the sinner while hating the
sin, nor the advice of Roger Hurding, a modern writer on
Christian counselling, that we should avoid '"summing up" other
people in a dismissive way'[13] was being followed.

In a situation where we refer to someone as 'a bully' we are
not just giving that person a 'label', but one which carries
strong moral disapproval. It would be better to refer to 'a person who exhibits bullying/racist behaviour' rather than to 'a

bully' or 'a racist'. By labelling people we appear to dismiss them; and we fail to offer any encouragement towards a change of behaviour. In trying to bring our prejudices into the light, we can start by being on the watch for language that both reveals and reinforces them.

• Questions about our principles and prejudices could be explored by using Story No. 2 'Tracy, Mandy, Martha and Jack', which follows at the end of this chapter. By exploring such issues in a group, people can help each other to find a way through today's 'moral maze', bring to light their unsuspected prejudices and find practical ways forward.

Two stories for discussion

2. Tracy, Mandy, Martha and Jack

TOPICS
• Moral principles
• Speaking frankly

Tracy and her husband and two small children live on an outer-city estate, where they attend a local church. Tracy has a former school friend, Mandy, who is a lone mother with a one-year-old daughter, Martha. Mandy has recently moved to live near Tracy and wants them to see each other and do things together. As far as Tracy can see, Mandy 'used' Martha's father, Jack, to enable her to conceive, but has never wanted to live with him. She now expects him to help by giving her money, but does not let him have any real part in Martha's life — except when she is in need of a baby-sitter.

Although Mandy puts on a convincing front and appears outwardly to be managing well, she is lonely, often gets depressed and badly needs someone to talk to. But Tracy is finding it difficult to listen to Mandy's troubles, because she feels strong disapproval of the whole course of action that has led to the present situation. She thinks Mandy has brought her present problems upon herself, behaved wrongly in the past, is still behaving wrongly towards Jack and is depriving Martha of a father. She believes that Mandy needs a change of heart at a deep level, but is unsure how to help her. She does not want to imply that she approves of Mandy's behaviour, but equally she does not want to risk losing their friendship through appearing cold and critical — especially as she is aware that she too has sometimes been guilty of 'using' other people.

Discussion

1 Should Tracy speak frankly to Mandy?
2 How should Tracy behave towards Mandy, in order to give her the support she needs, without compromising her own principles?

3. Pauline, John, Susan and Nic

TOPICS
* Boundaries:
  – how can I balance family, job and caring for others?
  – can a professional relationship be a friendly one as well?
* Being truthful
* Step-parents and step-children

Susan, a woman in her mid-thirties, had an attack of toothache. Her dentist, Pauline, agreed to fit her in for an appointment at the end of the day, after her assistant had gone home. Pauline had been Susan's dentist for several years and they had become friendly.

About five years ago Pauline married John, a businessman fifteen years older than herself, divorced with a teenage son. They had a baby, Lucy, now aged three. John has a job some distance away, has to go to work very early and gets back quite late in the evening. So he and Pauline have had very little time together recently. He only sees Lucy at weekends and is so tired that he is often impatient with her. He has no energy to help Pauline round the house. She is longing to have another child, but John does not want any more babies and they never have a chance to talk about it properly.

John's son, Nic, aged nineteen, comes to them for most weekends. He is big physically, talks a lot and altogether dominates everything. He has no friends locally, so never goes out. He likes teasing Pauline, saying, 'Well, how many people did you give toothache to this week, Pauline?' She wants to tell him she does not find this funny. But she feels it is important not to quarrel with him, because she knows he has been badly hurt in the past and needs a secure, welcoming home.

Susan hadn't seen Pauline for some time and before leaving she asked her how things were going for her these days. Pauline then poured out all her problems, to which Susan responded as best she could — though she wanted to get away because she had left her teenage daughter alone at home.

Discussion

1   What issues about caring for other people are raised for you by this story?

2   What do you think were Pauline's main problems? What were her main needs?

3   What feelings might Pauline's problems unlock in Susan (sad, angry, worried, disturbed by her own memories, itching to give advice and solve things, bewildered, impatient)?

4   Could Susan help any more in the future? Or did Pauline need professional help?

5   Should Susan suggest another time for Pauline to continue talking? (She might not want to make a big future commitment of time. She might prefer not to be on such intimate terms with her dentist – she'd rather keep it 'professional'. She might realize that she felt too involved and emotional – in various ways – to be able to help Pauline to find a new perspective. She might decide that Pauline ought to find someone else to help who would be more appropriate/more skilled.)

6   What were Susan's needs? Were they getting in the way of her listening to Pauline?

7   How could Susan most helpfully show Pauline that she cares?

CARING COMMUNITIES

'Commitment to community issues by local churches ... is a valuable springboard for mission. Those outside the church would want to help, and would enter an environment where Christian commitment and action were already at work.' (Dr David Hope)[1]

'Each community contains its own leaders, though their intelligence is often trampled on ... the Christian approach is to build up confidence in these people.' (Bishop David Sheppard)[2]

'The accountants have won, but missed the point. Our deepest need is not money, but a sense of belonging.' (Michael Bywater)[3]

'The church that helps'

How is a local church to decide its priorities? If resources of time and energy are limited, which is to come first: individual support or community schemes to make people's lives better? In practice the distinctions disappear. It is in caring for individuals that the need to take corporate action is uncovered. Then church members put their energy into community projects, through which many more people will feel they belong and are supported. Through such activities people can do useful and creative things, together with others, and find a wider perspective than that of their own problem-ridden street. A sense of hope and purpose begins to liberate their lives.

This chapter begins by describing in some detail two places where, in different ways, the real welfare issues affecting local people are massive and urgent. It then looks more briefly at some varied ideas that have been put into action by other churches.

Building community in Braxton

Harry is a minister in Braxton, a former mining village in the Midlands, with a population of about 3,500. When he came there five years ago, he found a small but faithful church congregation, set among a community that was steadily losing its heart, because the mine was being run down.

The colliery had been opened in the early 1920s, rapidly turning a small rural village into a thriving town. People seeking jobs in the mine came to Braxton from all over the country. The colliery built estates of housing, all in straight streets, rigidly demarcated into areas for managers, deputies, face workers and then for the majority of surface workers. The colliery had exercised a lot of control over people's lives, but in exchange it looked after you: there would be care for you in old age and a job for your son. And the 'Miners' Welfare' provided a social meeting place and focus for the community.

During the early 1990s the mine was gradually run down and has now closed. Most of the houses are now owned by a housing association which does not have enough money to keep them in good repair. There are many problems:

- Depression and hopelessness among men, who are mostly unemployed. Whereas often their wives have been able to

find part-time work, in some cases doing several part-time jobs at once, men feel that only a full-time job is a real job.
- Isolation. There are a few buses to the nearest small town, but none to any other town or city. So unless you have a car, shopping is limited and getting to the benefit office and job centre can be difficult.
- As a result of the isolation, people tend to have a narrow viewpoint.
- Boredom and hopelessness among the young, resulting in drug taking and vandalism.

When he arrived Harry saw the building up of community as the need he must tackle most urgently. He concentrated first on getting to know and make connections with all the local groups: the social workers, doctors and health visitors, the schools, the sporting clubs, the police, the pubs, all the voluntary groups – and many more. Then he set about launching 'Braxton Community Forum', in which about seventy groups are represented and which has since initiated many varied projects. The most successful has been Resources And Help for Unemployed in Braxton (RAHUB), which has steadily expanded and now employs three paid staff and many volunteers and offers a wide variety of courses and projects.

Harry believes that success in community development depends on several factors:

- Listening to find out people's real needs.
- Drawing in many people to take part – so that a project is owned by the community and is not just one person's hobby. *'My idea has to become our idea.'*
- Making a clear assessment of available skills, among those who are or might be involved.
- Above all persuading people to believe that they have the power to make change – in their own lives and in the community.

Harry has particularly encouraged all the members of the church congregation to be involved directly in caring for each other and for those around them. He has set up what he calls 'crisp organization and systems', which help everything to run smoothly. (We shall return to these in Chapter 8, page 145.)

Harry finds that people have a great need for the good news that 'God values people'. Every activity that helps people to believe they have worth is the work of Christ, and is both evangelism and pastoral care – even if it is not known by those names.

Building community in Long Copse

When Naomi came to St Flack's as minister she found a community struggling with poverty, isolation, drugs, crime, and a sense of hopelessness. The church stands on the edge of Long Copse Estate and also cares pastorally for two other big housing estates, built in the 1950s, on the edge of a large city, in what is now 'an area of particular economic and social deprivation'. The population is 8,000, of whom more than three-quarters live on benefit. Of the men, half are unemployed, of the women, more than one-third. The crime rate is high: stealing cars and motorcycles, burglary, vandalism, arson. There is open sale of drugs. People are afraid to go out at night and most families leave one member in the house at all times, especially as they cannot afford house insurance. There is a high rate of domestic violence against women. Old people are intimidated. The police on the beat are constantly frustrated and have low morale.

There are no leisure facilities nearer than the city centre which is four miles away. There are buses, but they are expensive. Few people have cars. Credit is almost unobtainable. Loan sharks operate, with violent retribution for non-payers. The bad reputation of the estates makes job seeking difficult for those who live on them.

There had been a long gap since the last minister left, after his home had been repeatedly broken into and the church had been vandalized. The church hall had been attacked and wrecked during one summer night and had then been out of use for many months. The congregation had kept going none the less, faithfully and against great odds. They continued to meet in the church, a building which had been put up at the same time as the estates — an austere concrete cube with a mass of glass in its construction, much of which was destroyed at the time that the hall was vandalized.

In this situation Naomi wondered where to begin. 'You just have to start where you are and do what you can.' Soon after her arrival she organized a weekend church conference. To this conference were invited, in addition to church members, a wide range of people involved in the community.

The conference decided that priority must be given to the needs of the children on the estates. More than one-third of the population were aged sixteen and under. A high number were on the Child Protection Register, there was much truancy, and many children were banned from secondary school. There was also bullying in school and on the way to and from school. Quite young children were involved in vandalism, burglary and harassment of old people.

Very little leisure activity of any kind was available for young people, least of all anything enjoyable and productive. Children, therefore, were identified as a particularly deprived group. Five aims were drawn up, to enable the children and young people:

- To have fun and receive stimulus which they do not get at home or school, and to widen their experience.
- To receive encouragement from a stable group of kindly volunteers in the background, including older people who could play a 'grandparent' role.
- To be given the feeling that they are each valuable, which would help them to value each other.

- To co-operate with each other and with adults, and to understand the benefits of communal activity.
- To think for themselves and make decisions about what they are doing.

Activities for children could not be started until there was a place in which they could happen. The process of getting the church hall back into working order had to be set in hand urgently — and this meant launching an ambitious appeal, with all the work entailed in approaching individuals, trusts, churches and companies.

For the appeal to succeed, its aims had to be specific and 'possible'. A wide range of people and groups were consulted — including the clergy of all the denominations, city councillors, Social Services, the schools, the police, journalists, many voluntary organizations, including the Long Copse Advice Centre, the Credit Union and the NSPCC. The money was raised, the church hall was refurbished and made as vandal-proof as possible.

Still more fund-raising was necessary, however, as a range of activities for youngsters began to be developed, with professional help being bought in as it was needed. Three years later, there are Boys and Girls Soccer Clubs; a Saturday Club; Summer Playschemes; a Teenage Active Group — which runs weekends away on a farm in the Lake District or a Youth Hostel in Lincolnshire; and Junior Church on Sunday mornings. There is also close liaison with the local authority's Play Group and the Girl Guide, Brownie and Rainbow packs, all of which meet in the church hall.

This is a success story so far, but it has been achieved at the cost of huge commitment and hard work by a few people. There has never been *enough* help. 'Everything is very fragile,' Naomi says. Yet she also wrote in a recent Newsletter to the parish, 'I love being your minister.' She has to do too much of the work with children herself, on top of the regular everyday involvement of a minister. 'My day begins with prayer in church and then goes on with listening and ends with listening. I do try to pay attention to what is going on in people's lives ... your life ... whether you are old or young, happy or sad. Someone described the job as "lurking with intent" and that seems about it. God's love, visible in us all in the parish of St Flack, is my intent.'

So the everyday work of individual pastoral care goes on and Naomi now has plans to recruit others to share the visiting and follow-up in connection with funerals and baptisms, home communions and friendship for those who are housebound. But the needs of the area are so great that individual care can never be enough. Naomi believes that improving the 'structures' and building 'corporate care' – so as to give hope to the next generation – are essential if God's love is to be shown forth in ways that make a difference.

Community projects

We shall now take a brief look at a few of the hundreds of projects, in all their varety, in which local churches are actively involved.

- A historic city-centre church in the West Country has been transformed into a Day Care Centre for the homeless, with a furniture recycling workshop, counselling service and food voucher scheme. 'Homelessness is not just a problem in London: it occurs also in pretty and historic cities like ours ... Once again Christian compassion and fellow feeling have responded in the most practical way to human need and to marginalised people.'[4]
- 'We felt that the churches were not as involved in the community as they should be.' A Christian coffee shop and bookshop were opened in a local shopping centre, with further plans in view for a drop-in centre for young people, where counselling will be provided.[5]

- In a country town in the Midlands a derelict listed building, a former manse which is owned by the local Baptist church, is starting a new life as a church drop-in centre. The church has managed to raise £350,000 to make this possible.[6]

- A minister who gave up a well-paid job with a large merchant bank in exchange for Christian ministry in an inner-city area has put his financial knowledge to good use by organizing a credit union. He says that this has helped to improve the lives of hundreds of people. 'In the past I could do deals involving millions of pounds and it would not noticeably affect anybody's life. Now, I enjoy the opportunity to see lives transformed. I see people finding hope and dignity and beginning to discover faith, through understanding they are a child of God.'[7]

- One church has led a scheme to build a Community Centre to serve a densely populated local area. 'The centre is vitally needed to provide a facility for ordinary people to do ordinary things. We hope it will be used to provide a place for young people to go and things for them to do, groups for parents and children and for the elderly – and possibly a doctor's surgery for people who cannot easily get to the main health centre.'[8] Some of the money for this project has come from a Foundation set up by a Church of England bishop with the aim of helping projects such as this to get started: 'The ethos of the Foundation is that the Church should make a real contribution to the social needs of the entire community.'

- The Grapevine Centre was born out of the desire of a relatively small Christian fellowship to make tangible its concern for the unemployed, through the provision of skills training and non-judgemental pastoral care. 'The Centre was financed jointly by our local United Reformed Church and the Manpower Services Commission ... It was soon apparent that what many users valued most was the sense of support, understanding and acceptance that existed in the "micro-society" of the Centre. Any hesitation about the church "tag" which the project carried was soon overcome by the lack of any overt or covert pressure to be a Christian. What became evident to those of us involved was how vulnerable every human being can be in particular circumstances and how fragile a veneer is the impression we all try to give that we are coping. Such was the church fellowship's belief that the centre was meeting pastoral needs that it raised the money to continue the work after the grant-aid from the MSC expired.'[9]

- 'The Well came into being following a survey of Asian families in our area of the city to establish what needs the church could help to meet. The almost unanimous response was for an advice centre ... At the heart of our work is a belief that Jesus commanded us to love our neighbour as ourselves ... we see this as an act of evangelism and hope that through the love people experience at The Well they will want to know more about the Christian faith for themselves. We do a lot of listening and only discuss religion when a client brings up the subject.'[10]

- In one village a new room for community use has been created within the parish church. 'Ever since we lost our village school in the early eighties, we have lamented its going, not least because it had doubled as a village hall and meeting place. Several people suggested that the north aisle of the church could be developed creatively to meet the needs of the youth group. The idea took off and an appeal for £30,000 was launched. A year later the pews had came out and the room was ready. The first activity it hosted was a children's holiday club ... For those of us most closely involved there has been the quiet but exciting conviction that the good hand of our God has been with us in it all.'[11]

- Members of 'Churches Together' in a northern city were determined to do something for homeless and lonely people. Within a year a drop-in centre had been opened in a large Victorian church hall. 'Now nearly six years later, the building is transformed. The hall has a warm friendly atmosphere, where guests and volunteers chat over tea. About 80 people a day enjoy the three-course lunch on offer, upstairs there is a clothing store and a bathroom and shower and a couple of rooms for people to go for private chats or advice ... Perhaps the largest single group who come are those who have nothing else to do. Many of them live in rooms in multiple-occupancy houses, sharing kitchens and bathrooms with people they don't trust. Most of them have given up all hope of getting a job. They are despondent, bored and lonely and just managing to survive on their income support ... The aim of the Centre is to provide a warm, caring environment for people in need and to offer them love, God's love, expressed as practical help – food, clothing, medical care, advice, comfort or just somewhere "to be".'[12]

- The Church Restaurant Project is to be found in what was once an 800-year-old coaching inn in a large town. It is run by a Project Team which involves local churches of all denominations. 'This is being developed as a centre of Christian hospitality and witness through events and exhibitions, the use of its rooms for local business meetings, three restaurants, a Tradecraft shop and a Christian bookstore ... I have never seen a church-led project which has generated such enthusiastic support ... the dedication and professionalism of our team has already impressed many who thought churches stood for pious incompetence and irrelevance.'[13]

- 'Recognizing the needs in our area, it is amazing what can be achieved by love and by working together as a body. It can have an effect on problems like homelessness and poverty. In our parish there is a redundant pub which has been bought by the diocese for conversion into a church. It will include other facilities that will help a fairly poor community. There will also be provision for a caretaker, so it will become a home for a couple as well and provide a job and security for them.'

• 'The vicar of a rural parish wants to use the buildings that
were once a church school and now stand empty to give
summer holidays to children from the city. A strong faction
in the village is vigorously opposed to this plan: they
maintain that "the presence of these children will be
disturbing, might even be dangerous and will require us to
help entertain them." The issue is dividing the village.'[14] Some
local people think the vicar should aim to keep the peace and
start no more such schemes in the future. Others feel he is
right to offer care for those city children, even if it is at the
cost of some disturbance to his own parishioners – but
wonder if he will be able to make them see their duty to
help these 'neighbours' who live outside their own small area.
'If he can do so, he will have cared for us in an important
sense – although some may feel that he has done the opposite
and failed to care for them in the way they wished.'

Some conclusions

1   Ambitious projects can succeed, provided they are
    designed to meet real needs, planned with forethought and
    underpinned by prayer.
2   The most effective care often results from co-operation –
    when a church or group of churches works together with
    the statutory services or with existing voluntary bodies.
3   Community projects generate enthusiasm, a wider
    perspective and a spirit of teamwork which benefit those
    who give help as much as those who receive it.
4   On the other hand, there are people who, if they are
    asked to give care to those who do not 'belong' or
    conform, feel a threat to their personal sense of security.
    But they may also receive a challenge which, in the long
    run, helps them to grow.
5   Many people need various kinds of practical assistance, but
    many are also 'despondent, bored or lonely' and their

needs to belong, to be valued, to be given hope, are equally pressing.

6   Practical projects are uniquely effective in persuading people to take the Christian faith seriously. Church members who are seen giving generously of their time and commitment make an impression and people become open to the idea that the church might offer them something 'relevant' – even a purpose and meaning for their lives.

Story for discussion

4. Simon

TOPICS
* Care for the whole person
* Community action
* Pastoral care and evangelism
* Motives

Simon Adakah is a Methodist minister in Ghana. He writes: 'I was asked to take charge of a church whose own minister had left to do a year's course abroad. This church is situated in a rural community, in which fishing and farming are the main occupations. The people live in simple houses, without any social amenities. Although the residential areas on one side of the village had electricity, the village had none. The village's Chapel too was well lit, but the village itself was in total darkness.

'As soon as I took over, I asked the local church leaders how many of the village people belonged to the church. I was told there were only five. The church had been in the village for over forty years and yet only five people were in the church. The church had a membership of over four hundred, but almost all came from the residential areas. I suggested that it is the responsibility of the church to serve as the Light of the people.

'After discussing the situation, it was felt that the church would be more appreciated if it could do something practical to help the villagers. We thought of two things: Providing bathrooms for men and women and providing street lights. Next we consulted the Chief and his Elders about the plan to build public bathrooms. They were pleased with us and gladly showed us two possible places.

'But we kept the street lights secret from them, as we wanted to give the village a surprise which would be their Christmas gift. We bought six electric poles, got wires and fluorescent tubes and bulbs ready. On the 23rd December we got the youth wing of the church digging up holes and planting the poles in the main street. On the 24th the electricians completed the wiring and installing the tubes and bulbs. In the evening at 6.00 p.m. we went to the Chapel and put on its lights and then we came

out and switched on the lights in the streets. This was met by spontaneous and thunderous cheers by the villagers. The children shouted and jumped about in excitement. The Chief and his Elders came out from their houses and watched the glowing lights with amazement and appreciation.

'A week later a delegation from the village, led by the Chief, came to meet the church leaders. The Chief said: "Reverend Minister, and Leaders, we are indeed taken aback by this wonderful gesture of yours, by which you have turned our darkness into light. This your church has been here for forty years, but this is the first time that you have thought about us. Even though the Chapel is in the heart of the village, we have always looked upon the church as a community of inward-looking people. Today you have proved us wrong. We now see you as a caring church. I want to assure you that as from today I and the Elders and our families belong to the church."

'We thanked the Chief and said that all along we had been thinking of the village, but because our finances were not sound enough to do anything for them, it looked as if we did not care. We promised that we would now be going ahead to build the public bathrooms and offer any other help when need arose.

'The following Sunday the Chief and some of his Elders and their families came to church and they have continued to worship regularly since then.

'As a church we have learned that it is our duty to share what we have with those who have not. We now therefore collect clothes and other items which we supply to the children and needy people in the village. Members of the church have become more aware of their mission as a caring community.'

Discussion

1   In this account, how did the church understand its role as a 'caring community'? How did it see pastoral care?
2   What were the motives of (a) the church leaders in giving practical help to the village, and (b) the Chief and the villagers in joining the church?
3   How does 'pastoral care' relate to 'mission'?

MAKING PASTORAL CARE WORK

GETTING ORGANIZED

'I feel awkward about visiting someone unless I have been invited. You don't want to intrude. Of course it's different when there's a crisis.' (Church member)

'The whole scheme depends on a core of reliable retired people, who are fully committed and have time.' (Minister)

'Love shone out of his filing cabinets.' (From a tribute to a bishop on his retirement)[1]

'When I'm ill, I just want to be left alone.' (Church member)

Organizing

Most people dislike the idea of being 'organized'. We think of bossy people trying to make us do things we do not want to do and in ways that are not our natural ways. The word 'organization' suggests a large group in the secular world of business and government. And yet we have plenty of 'organization' in our churches. Look at the noticeboard of any local church: there are rotas for coffee-making and flower-arranging and cleaning; lists of stall-holders for the church bazaar and of leaders of House Groups, Junior Church, Youth Fellowship.

The word 'organize' was originally connected with the idea of a 'tool', something that is useful, something that enables one to do a particular job. So the question is not whether we want organization, but rather, do we have the best kinds and levels of organization? Do we have the best 'tools' to enable us to carry out the proper work of our particular local church?

In the apostolic church, as the community grew, it became difficult to care for everyone adequately and in a manner that was seen to treat everyone equally. So they took some definite steps to make sure that everyone who needed care would receive it and that the work of caring was shared out. They 'got organized' (Acts 6:1–6).

Basic questions

Today, when a local church begins to organize 'care', some questions arise at once.

- Who does the church care for? Everyone in its area or only church members? Is it best to concentrate on certain groups, on those with known links with the church or, deliberately, on 'outsiders'?
- What are people's real needs? How much 'care' goes on already? What is already being done – by 'official' groups or through unofficial 'networks'? What are the gaps? It may be necessary to conduct a survey to find out.
- How can confidentiality be respected? What about the times when there are conflicts between the demands of family, neighbours and work? How should people be guided on these questions?

Help with exploring such issues is given in Section Three.

Getting started

There are several broad models for supplying 'pastoral care'. The main ones are described below.

1 No formal structure: Neighbours and ministers respond to needs and requests as best they can. Neighbours pass on some information to ministers and do a lot themselves, but there are 'gaps'.

2 'Street warden' structure: The area is divided up and each street or district is looked after by a church member, who passes information to ministers when necessary – and when they remember.

3 'Pastoral team': A group of people, lay and ordained, are formed into a team. They are trained and supported, so that they can respond to needs and requests.

4 'Virtual teams': This model is described by a minister whose church is in a large village. 'Teams just arise, as they are needed and lasting as long as they are needed. A team consists of those friends and neighbours who are involved in a situation naturally. They keep me informed and involve me when I am required. I feel that a more organised "pastoral care team" runs the dangers of bringing in the "wrong" people, (people who have needs of their own to work through), is excluding of others and, once formed, is difficult to change. As I see it "virtual teams" work better!'

5 Using groups: In some churches pastoral care is mostly done through the groups that meet regularly, such as 'fellowship groups' or 'house groups'. 'In our church every member is assigned to a group, though people vary as to whether they attend the meetings. Group leaders, too, vary as to how well they care for their members. But on the whole it does ensure that no one is left out.'

6 Using elders, pastoral leaders, pastoral visitors, pastoral assistants or overseers: Each leader is made responsible for

caring for perhaps ten people or families who belong
to the congregation – or sometimes for a task, such as
organizing the visiting of the house-bound or leading the
Sunday School or Junior Church. The leaders themselves
are usually put on someone else's list, so that they too
receive care. Leaders may be carefully selected or it may
be a case of looking round for anyone who is willing to
take the job on. Usually leaders meet together regularly
and the provision of training – in some form – is seen
as important.

Many churches combine a 'street warden' type of system, which
may be more or less complex in its structure, with a 'pastoral
team'. There are many variations on all these themes, according
to local need.

Some local churches

We shall now look at some local churches, to find out what
their practice is and whether it works. What is successful? What
is difficult? What changes are planned? What aspects of their
experience might relate to our own needs?

Middleford – an estate on the edge of a Midlands city
Chidbury – a country town
Nolling – a large suburban town
Pytchford – three churches and a large pastoral team
Pinwell – a Methodist church in a country town
Bensdown – a mostly affluent suburban area
Two groups of rural churches – Slipstock and Binkley-on-the-
Hill; Todfield, Rudwell and Little Loxbury

Middleford: 'Results coming slowly'
We start in Middleford, a Midlands city, where Julie is the vicar
of one of the parish churches, St Andrew's, which covers a

population of 6,000. The church building — a 1960s structure, with the look of a 'prefab' about it — is placed on the edge of a big estate where many very deprived families live. When Julie arrived in Middleford a year ago, she found that most families on the estate were struggling with their own day-to-day problems and were either apathetic about or resistant to any attempts by others to regulate their lives. For instance there is a part-time community worker, employed by 'Churches Together in Middleford', who gives most of his available time to the estate. He has tried to set up a 'foster granny' scheme, linking children with lonely older people, but has had limited success.

On the other hand, some of the older women — mainly those who live alone — have already made friends with a child 'unofficially'. This has happened as a result of a scheme in which older people go in to the First School, to help by hearing children read. Julie thinks these links work because they have arisen out of another activity, rather than being set up deliberately. She also discovered that some families were running their own informal 'care' scheme, in order to make sure that their elderly neighbours were not neglected. It seemed best to support this, rather than to organize anything else.

PROBLEMS

There are many problems on the estate, about which Julie feels that almost nothing is being done by the statutory authorities, such as the following:

- A large number of young single parents, many of whom feel isolated and are struggling to cope.
- A high level of unemployment, since the most usual former sources of jobs, such as farming and building, have collapsed.
- Complicated families: often there are three or four surnames in one family.
- Boys aged between twelve and fifteen who have been excluded from school and form gangs.

- Small children who are out of hand, because their parents/ mothers do not know how to bring them up.
- Drugs and alcohol, which are definitely there, although so far they have not caused visible problems.

NEW DIRECTIONS
Here are some of the initiatives Julie has taken:

- She has formed a 'ministry team' of six people, all from the estate, to help lead the main service on Sunday, chiefly by taking their turn at assisting with the chalice. She thinks you have to get people doing things first – even something very simple such as reading out a notice – then afterwards you can do the explaining and teaching. These 'pastoral assistants' meet with Julie about once every two months, mainly to discuss the Sunday worship. Julie hopes gradually to involve them in practical 'caring' as well.
- She has started a junior choir. This is popular – in spite of being quite demanding and disciplined, since they follow the procedures of the Royal College of Church Music.
- She arranges as many special services as possible – Mothering Sunday, Harvest, Christingle – almost any excuse will do – which she can publicize through the school, where she teaches RE. In these services she encourages as many people as possible to take an active part, especially through music. The local school knows about these opportunities and helps by providing some tuition and hiring out instruments.
- From time to time she asks lay people to speak in the Sunday service about something they know well – not a 'sermon'. Recently a member of the St John's Ambulance talked about service to the community; an elderly lady talked about her memories of being one of a family of eight living in Cornwall, with a widowed mother, and what their lives were like.

THE FUTURE

At the moment those who ask for baptism and marriage have to come to only one meeting beforehand: there are plans to offer better preparation. There is almost nothing for teenagers to do on the estate, so the church may try to start an after-school club and a drop-in centre for young people. But in making plans for the future Julie has to think carefully about her own priorities. For example, the local Volunteer Centre organizes a scheme for redistribution of furniture. The church (which in practice mostly meant the vicar) used to help by supplying household goods and small furnishings to people who needed them. Julie's own garage was filled with the furniture, until someone set fire to it. After that she decided that the personal cost to her of being involved in this project was too high.

Julie has found that most people living on the estate served by St Andrew's lack confidence in themselves and have little desire or energy to take action about anything. Many are caught in the 'poverty trap' and therefore have given up trying to do much for themselves. So she is careful to support, rather than undermine, anything, however modest, that people are doing. She is trying to build people's confidence, at least for those who come to church. She has begun the slow work of helping people to feel they are part of a church 'family', where they can contribute. She is encouraging any links that may be productive. She is working in collaboration with the nearby Methodist and Independent Evangelical churches and with whatever statutory help is available. She accepts that none of this is going to produce quick improvements or results that can easily be measured.

Chidbury: 'Church Neighbours'

Next we go to Chidbury, a country town with a population of about 7,000. In addition to the Anglican Parish Church of St Margaret's, there are Methodist and Roman Catholic churches and an active 'Churches Together' committee. The parish church has, over the last five years, made a determined effort to set up an organized pastoral care scheme to look after all church members.

HOW IT BEGAN

The church recently found itself in a crisis: the vicar was suddenly taken ill and had to be out of action for some weeks. This situation provided the immediate impetus for setting up a new pastoral care scheme.

NEEDS

There were some urgent needs:

• For care to be provided for all church members at least, rather than only for the relatively few families who happened to come to the vicar's attention.

Other needs were perhaps less obvious, but no less significant:

• The congregation needed to develop a stronger sense of being a community.
• Many people were in need of encouragement: because of having no job; because of feeling out of their depth as parents; or because of a sense of helplessness and inability to get anywhere in their lives.
• Some church members needed to be affirmed in their Christian discipleship: they needed help to believe that their own faithful effort, day by day, to follow Christ's teaching, is a powerful form of evangelism.
• Other church members needed help in deepening their commitment.

PREPARATION

One person, Kathleen, had the idea that if steps could be taken to fulfil the first, practical need, then the church would find that it was already some way towards meeting the others. Kathleen and her husband, who is a surveyor, are active lay members of St Margaret's. They have three children and Kathleen works part-time as a teacher. They both feel they have a calling to give their 'spare' time to their local church.

First Kathleen got together a small steering group to plan a visiting scheme. They agreed on a 'street warden' system, with the map of the parish divided into areas, and each area assigned to the care of one person or couple. Each of these 'church neighbours' would have a partner, with whom they could share and pray about their concerns. The title 'Church Neighbours' (or CNs) was agreed. (Other titles were considered but rejected, such as 'Street Wardens' – sounds too formal – and 'Good Neighbours' – sounds complacent.)

They devised a system for passing on, storing and using information – a system which is still evolving.

They worked out what the 'job' of being a 'church neighbour' would involve. The aim would be, initially at least, not to reach out to the 'unchurched', but to cover all those who already had some links with the church. The job of a CN would involve the following activities:

- To be aware of church members in your street and make friends with them.
- To visit the elderly, the newly baptized, the newly married, and anyone who is temporarily 'needy' in any way.
- To meet your prayer partner regularly (if possible in the church), to share concerns and pray together.
- To deliver baptism anniversary cards.
- To deliver communications from the church, such as invitations.
- To pass on information about house moves, illness, death, to the co-ordinator and the vicar.
- To arrange lifts.
- To attend three meetings a year.
- To remember the importance of confidentiality.

PEOPLE

The PCC accepted the scheme and Kathleen was appointed as 'co-ordinator'. She began identifying people who might become 'church neighbours'. The two essential qualities needed were a committed faith and an outgoing personality. A few people were obviously suitable, others had to be searched for. The vicar made the initial approach to individuals, being careful not to let people think they were being criticized because they had not been sufficiently neighbourly in the past or not in the right way. On the contrary the scheme was meant to encourage and support them.

It turned out in practice to be impossible to cover the whole parish, but it was felt to be better to have some gaps than to risk recruiting unsuitable people. The 'gap' areas are looked after by the ministers.

Just one year after the initial meeting the scheme was officially launched, with a special commissioning service on a Sunday morning, during which each 'Church Neighbour' stood up (so that they would be recognized) and made a commitment.

TRAINING AND SUPPORT
No one was to feel under pressure to do anything that was beyond them – either for reasons of time or lack of confidence. Nor were people to be persuaded to do things for which they had no aptitude.

No training was offered for CNs initially, as it was felt that people should not be told 'how', but should find their own style and methods. However, coffee evenings were held for the CNs once a month, so that they could discuss the scheme and share ideas and problems. About six months after the launch one training event was held on a Saturday, at which an outside consultant helped the CNs to reflect on their experience so far and make plans for the future. The scheme is prayed for at regular intervals in the intercessions in church on Sunday.

RELATING TO OTHER BODIES
1   Social Services: The town's Care Manager has made sure that a representative of the church is invited to any meetings in the town about 'Community Care'. This has ensured that social workers know about the church's scheme.

2   The rest of the churches: The scheme's co-ordinator belongs
     to the committee of 'Churches Together', so all the
     churches hear about the 'CN' scheme, even though each
     denomination organizes 'care' for its own members in its
     own way.

AFTER FOUR YEARS

- With hindsight, one year to prepare the scheme was not
  enough – especially to ensure that there would be proper
  support for all those involved.
- The scheme has got smaller. Several of the original team of
  CNs have dropped out and it has not been possible to find
  new ones. Recently the existing CNs have expressed a need
  for more coordination and support, but it has not been
  possible to develop this, because the parish is in a rather
  low state. Those who have dropped out seem to have been
  those who were weakest in their faith.
- The vicar has supported the scheme in theory, but in practice
  has found it difficult to work co-operatively. He does not
  always remember to pass on information – and this has
  hindered the working of the scheme. The structure needs to
  be changed so that it does not rely on faultless functioning
  by any one person.
- It has proved difficult to develop a completely satisfactory
  method for passing on information. People need to feel
  they can talk freely, knowing that what they say will not
  be repeated – therefore minimal records are kept. The
  co-ordinator keeps a list in a card index, which includes only
  the minimum of factual details about people. (If a list were
  to be kept on computer it would be necessary to comply
  with Data Protection regulations.)
- Some of the CNs very much want specific instruction. The
  question is being asked: 'is more training needed'?
- Most of the CNs have not managed to find a partner, so
  there has been a lack of collaboration, of support and of
  prayer. People do not yet know how to work in these ways.
  But these possibilities are still there as ideas which can be
  developed in the future.

CONCLUSION

There have been difficulties, but the basic structure is in place now and can be expanded – and made better – in future. At least now all church contacts are properly listed, not just scribbled in the vicar's notebook – or stored in his head.

Nolling: 'Friendly Faces'

On now to a suburban town, with a much larger population – about 17,000. Nolling lies on the edge of a large Midland city and has Anglican, Methodist, Baptist and Roman Catholic churches.

The Church of England parish has two churches, St Matthew's and St Julian's, with a total 'electoral roll' of 280, and is led by a team of ministers. Pastoral care is seen as the responsibility of the whole body, with the clergy in the team attending mainly to crisis situations and to outreach – which often includes ministry arising out of weddings, baptisms and funerals. Sheila, who is a curate in the team, says 'I feel that the most important role for me as a minister is to love and cherish the people who form the body, so that they in turn are strong enough to care for those outside.'

Three schemes are running at the moment which, in different ways, encourage people to care for their neighbours.

LAY PASTORS

A team has recently been formed made up of eight 'lay pastors', all regular members of one or other of the congregations. They were all chosen by the Team Rector, who looked for people with natural pastoral gifts who would benefit by being 'commissioned' in a formal way. A training programme was devised for them and they are now asking for some more training for particular situations – such as visiting families where a baby is to be baptized.

'A TUESDAY WELL SPENT'

This course in pastoral care is open to anyone who wants to become a more helpful 'neighbour'. The course is thorough – it has fourteen sessions, led by the ministry team and by some speakers from outside.

'FRIENDLY FACES'

An informal visiting team that was started by Jean, a member of the congregation who works as a community nurse. She is manager of an NHS scheme which supplies nursing care for housebound people. She found that, in addition to their need for nursing, clients often needed a friendly, listening ear. Three years ago she talked about this to one of the ministers, a meeting was held to see if there was enough interest – and 'Friendly Faces' was born. A small steering group was formed, which included Beth, a district midwife, who was, and is, the 'hub' of neighbourly care in the town. The whole congregation was told about the new scheme, so that it could be owned by everyone.

Volunteers to help were invited to come forward, ten people responded and a sheet of guidelines has been drawn up, so they know what is expected of them: 'Friendly Faces is a group of people who want to show they care by visiting others who would welcome it. We have to be careful not to offer the kind of advice that only experts should offer. If we think that expert advice is needed we should suggest that the person we are visiting speaks to a doctor or nurse or professional counsellor.' Confidentiality is emphasized and some practical tips are given. The visitors have a support meeting once a month. Most of them have been attending the 'Tuesday Well Spent' pastoral care course.

AFTER THREE YEARS

The scheme is still not well enough known in the community generally and does not any longer seem to be a central concern of the congregation; for example, it has become difficult to recruit new volunteer visitors. So thought is now being given to some fresh ideas:

• Explore linking up with local GP practices.
• Arrange for a slot on local radio and in the local press.

- Produce an attractive poster to go up in halls and waiting rooms.
- Put articles about the scheme in the church's newsletter.
- Mention the scheme more frequently in the Sunday intercessions in church.
- Make sure that each volunteer receives prayer support from someone else.

Pytchford: a large team

Jim is a keen member of a church in Pytchford. Ten years ago, when he retired early from running his own small business, one of the ministers asked him if he would be willing to set up and lead a 'pastoral team' in the parish. Here is how he went about it.

Ours is quite a large town: the population is about 12,000 and we have three churches, with a staff of only one full-time minister and one assistant – so they could not possibly do all the 'pastoral care' that is needed on their own. I had been living in Pytchford for many years and I knew a lot of people, so I began by making a list of those who I thought would be suitable and approaching each of them in turn.

I immediately ran into a difficulty: people were reluctant about accepting the invitation to join the proposed Pastoral Team. They produced all sorts of reasons.

'Surely it's the clergy's job?' – some were unsure whether it was right for 'lay people' to undertake what they had always seen as the role of the clergy.

'I really haven't time!' – in one form or another this was the most frequent 'excuse', but I discovered that it often masked other anxieties, such as: 'I'm not qualified to do this ... I wouldn't know what to do ... I haven't anything in common with old people ... I've my own family to look after.'

I had to listen to and respect these misgivings – that was my own new lesson in 'pastoral care'. In the end several people agreed to come to a meeting and as a result they all decided to give it a try. Since then they have become enthusiastic ... really I can say they have become dedicated.'

From the beginning there has been a good balance of men and women – whereas in many places it is usual to recruit mainly women. This is probably because they *started by recruiting men*. There were the minister and Jim and two or three other men – then in some cases their wives joined later. But it *started* with men, so it has always been seen as an activity that is very appropriate for them.

The scheme grew from that original half dozen into a large team of twenty-six visitors. Jim acted as co-ordinator of the scheme for the first three years. His main job was to match 'visitors' to 'clients'. This was often quite tricky.

- Occasionally a person objected to a lay visitor, but more often people said, reasonably, that they would prefer a visitor of the same sex, or of roughly the same age group: 'I don't want youngsters visiting me!' This preference has had to be respected – although Jim finds that when a friendship does develop between a younger and an older person, it can be rewarding for both of them.
- Sometimes it became apparent after a few weeks or months that the relationship was uncomfortable and a friendship had not developed. 'Redeployment' was necessary. This had to be handled with tact, so that neither of them felt they had failed, but at the same time the visitor was encouraged to reflect on the experience and learn from it.

From time to time it happens that a visitor gets into a state of some distress: 'I can't cope. She wants me to go every day', or, 'He always moans and grumbles the whole time ... it's getting me down', or, 'She regards me as her servant – do this, do that'. Sometimes the problem sounds trivial: 'I don't like cats and her moggie just loves jumping on to my lap', but if the visitor or 'client' are feeling upset it has to be taken seriously. Jim found he had to be both counsellor and diplomat.

Once the scheme was established Jim handed over its day-to-day running to Betty, who is a retired hospital sister and ideal for the job of co-ordinator, as she has the right skills and she has time. She now does most of the work, but Jim remains as a kind of overseer. They co-operate happily.

They no longer have any problems in finding people for the pastoral team. 'We have become expert in spotting possible people – and then we pounce on them! If they seem interested, Betty arranges a time for a proper talk.' Some people do gossip, so confidentiality is stressed. They find it best to keep the minimum of records in a card index held by Betty. Only names, addresses and the dates of visits or of any other action taken are noted.

Jim says, 'We have never gone in for formal training, because all our visitors are mature, experienced people. The simple friendliness we offer is felt to be important: we don't want to become "experts". For instance, questions such as when to call in a "professional" or how to set reasonable time limits seem to be solved by common sense. However, the whole Pastoral Care Team has a quarterly meeting at which they can share any problems. People come up with good new ideas too: last Christmas for the first time we distributed flowers and greetings cards to people who live alone or have been recently bereaved. We felt quite overwhelmed by the letters of gratitude we received afterwards.'

Lately they have developed groups of visitors who have particular skills in looking after those who are ill and those who are bereaved. Recently they decided to do something practical to help those who are lonely: so they have started a monthly parish lunch for elderly people – and this is going well.

After the main service on Sunday morning, Jim takes extended Holy Communion to a few of the most housebound people. At first some were worried by the idea of a lay person doing this, but were quite satisfied when it was properly explained to them. However Jim says there are two people who still feel they only want to receive Communion from someone who is ordained.

Names of people to visit are given to the team by ministers or by neighbours and friends or – now that the team is well known and trusted – people ask for a visitor for themselves. Jim and Betty then try to assess their needs, which is sometimes easy, sometimes difficult.

For non-urgent situations the process they have developed over the years goes like this:

1   Vicar, other clergy, Jim or Betty are given bare details: name and address and reason for wanting a visitor.
2   Assessment is carried out through a joint visit to the person by Jim and Betty.
3   They discuss any difficulties, bringing in clergy if necessary.
4   A visitor is allocated and given a thorough and helpful briefing by Betty.

When a situation is urgent (a sudden emergency, such as death, acute illness or a 'wedding crisis') it is usually dealt with by the clergy. Later, if needed, the procedure above can be used, 'to make sure that the person is not abandoned – simply because everyone thinks the person has come through and will be all right now.'

JIM'S FINAL WORD

'Those who do so much caring need to be cared for themselves. I have to make sure that all team members find really adequate personal support. The quarterly meetings are helpful and they know that Betty, myself and the clergy are always ready to talk with them individually.' There are bound to be difficulties in an organized scheme, but by careful thought, love and prayer they can be overcome, so that everyone benefits.

Pinwell Methodist Church: a pastoral visitor for every member

Mary is a Minister in Local Appointment, in charge of the Methodist church in a middle-sized country town. The church has 60 members and a longer list of 120 people who are connected in various ways. Everyone is assigned to a 'Pastoral Visitor'. These visitors are recruited by Mary, with help from the Church Council. Each looks after a small group of people, which varies in number from two to twelve, though six seems to work best.

MARY'S REFLECTIONS

'I see it as important that everyone has a pastoral visitor, including the pastoral visitors themselves. I would like more men to be visitors: at the moment only one out of 14 is a man. The Pastoral Visitors get together twice a year: at this meeting problems can be shared, but it is not the same as "training" as such. I recently organised a course in "listening skills", which the visitors could join if they wished, and I am beginning to think that some more training would be helpful.'

Bensdown: The Shepherds

The church in the centre of this relatively affluent suburban area has a congregation that includes some talented and energetic people, who often initiate projects.

One example is the organized pastoral care scheme, known as 'The Shepherds'. Helen, who is an enthusiast, had the idea originally and then, with the backing of the church's Outreach Committee, set it up. She now acts as 'shepherd's warden' or co-ordinator. She has recruited the 'shepherds' by asking for volunteers. They concentrate on the welcoming of new arrivals. No formal training is arranged for them, but they meet occasionally to share experiences.

There is also an informal network, run by some ladies who have been doing it for a long time, for visiting those who are sick and housebound, including some of those living in the many nursing homes and homes for the elderly in this area.

Some rural churches: special problems and opportunities

Slipstock and Binkley-on-the-Hill

Cara and her husband recently moved from South London to the small village of Slipstock. The minister here is Roger, who is also in charge of four other villages. Cara soon discovered that Roger was worried about the considerable deprivation in these isolated communities. Much of this was invisible, which meant that pastoral care was patchy. Neighbours were helpful to each other, but there were still people who felt isolated and lonely.

Here is Cara's account of what happened next.

When I was working in a city area I helped with a well-developed lay-training scheme, which gave me useful experience in recruiting and training lay people. I was enthusiastic when I was invited to help in forming a pastoral team to cover our group of villages. We began by asking around for names of people who might be suitable to join. Several people's names kept coming, so Roger approached them. We decided not to offer any formal training for the visitors at this stage, though we did hold 'support meetings' quite frequently. We find our 'clients' by a variety of informal means – by 'networking' I suppose. Basic information about them is kept by Roger.

After a time the need became apparent for some kind of 'authorization' for the visitors: they needed it for greater confidence, the 'clients' needed it for reassurance. Roger was told that if they wanted formal accreditation they must do some training. None of the courses that were available seemed quite suitable and anyway the 'venues' were too distant. So Cara set up a tailor-made course, to develop the knowledge and skills the visitors needed.

A BASIC COURSE IN A RURAL AREA
This course was similar to the one described in Chapter 11. These are Cara's comments on it:

We made sure that our course would include items that are specially relevant to our villages:

- Each small community has its own character and within each there are different groups with different needs, such as 'incomers', 'old villagers', those who are unemployed, those who have taken early retirement, young families, farming families, members of ethnic minorities, teenagers, those who care at home for elderly or handicapped relatives, people who live in isolated situations and do not have cars.

- 'Community Care' is often deficient in small villages. But we need to know about all the local resources that are available to help people – through both local authority structures and voluntary groups.

- We need to be sure that we understand the particular role of our ordained minister, who lives in Slipstock but has to try to give equal attention to people in Binkley.

Then Cara came across an unexpected difficulty. In Binkley there was a group of women who were already giving 'pastoral care' to some elderly neighbours. Cara explained to them that the vicar wanted to make this 'official' and provide them with some training. They seemed resistant and after a bit of probing she discovered why: they had recently visited another parish where there was a 'Pastoral Team'. Its members were much more 'religious' than they were and they were frightened that they would be pushed into *that* by 'training'. Cara was able to allay this fear and they eventually agreed that they did need training in supporting young parents and with guidelines for visiting – although they still felt doubts as to whether the latter needed expert advice: 'you just call round in a friendly way'.

Six months later all those doing visiting on behalf of the church had been through the basic training course and a short ceremony for commissioning the visitors was held. Cara reports: 'Everyone was pleased about this. The visitors now see, more clearly than before, that they go as representatives of the whole church – rather than as private individuals. And those cared for can be sure that "the church" knows about them and will look after them.'

THE FUTURE

- Better sharing of information and keeping of records are needed, but without breaking confidentiality. At the moment when people see a pastoral need, they are often unsure who they should contact and what information they should pass on. Working out a system and making sure everyone understands it is the next task.
- Finding out what the young people in a small village want and whether more can be done to involve them in church life will be important. They tend just to drift away, but they are badly needed if village communities are to survive and flourish.

Todfield, Rudwell and Little Loxbury

Paul is the minister in another group of small villages. He has recently started a 'Pastoral Visitors Team', along the same lines as Slipstock. But he began differently, by asking for volunteers. He felt encouraged that eight people signed up, but he wished the list had not included Mrs G., who had always done a lot of visiting and saw herself as a 'lady bountiful'. Paul felt this might create future problems. He hopes, however, that belonging to the team will help her to understand that 'pastoral care is not something we – the lucky ones – do for others who are less lucky, but something we all do for each other.'

Paul held a meeting for the people who had expressed interest. He told them that the most urgent need was for regular visiting of elderly people who could not get out very much. He gave them some practice in better listening. He explained some of the difficulties that might arise – such as over-dependence. He gave them information about other resources and also a list of each others' addresses. Then he paired each of them with a 'client'. He knew all the elderly people quite well himself and explained to each of them that a different person would soon start coming.

THE FUTURE
Paul thinks the following points will prove important:

- Finding someone else to run the scheme in due course – including arranging frequent support meetings for the visitors – and then extending it to newcomers and 'baptism families'.
- Making better use of the church hall in Todfield, perhaps for a meeting and mid-week service for parents with small children and as a place where lonely older people could meet.
- Remembering in planning any project to arrange lifts for those without cars.

SOME CONCLUSIONS ABOUT GETTING ORGANIZED
Every church needs:

- To devise an information system that is easy to understand so that it is not abandoned almost at once because it is so complicated. The problem is that even the best systems depend on people being efficient. A computer database is no better than a scribbled notebook at producing information, if the information has not been put into it. In the end every scheme depends on people being sensitively observant of

what is going on around them and careful to pass on what
they see to the right person. We have to accept that no
human arrangement can be — or remain — perfectly tidy.
Networks overlap, or leave empty areas; people do not stay
in the same place, but move — or die; lists soon become out
of date; people are forgetful. There are organizations whose
business it is to advise on organizing.[2] But every method
has to be tested in practice to see how well it works and
gradually improved in the light of experience.

- To co-operate with other people and other groups that are
  caring for people.
- To support informal caring networks.
- To seek out and encourage people who have time, gifts,
  resources and enthusiasm which could be used for the good
  of everyone — but may lack confidence in themselves.
- To allow enough time to prepare and pray about the setting
  up of a new scheme.
- To accept that schemes must continue to be worked at and
  results may be slow; but to be thankful for even small signs
  of progress.
- To work at combining effective communication with respect
  for confidentiality.
- To believe that difficulties can be overcome.
- To consider the best use of the time and energy of ministers,
  especially where they have oversight of several separate
  communities.
- To remember the particular needs of people living in
  villages, urban estates and suburbs.
- To remember that it is risky for any scheme to be dependent
  on one person. It is better to build a team.
- To nurture and strengthen people's faith: this produces the
  most committed volunteers.
- To believe that training can help people to become more
  effective in their caring, but also to listen to those who
  have a healthy distrust of experts.

- To give clear guidelines to people who undertake caring in the name of the church, so that they are sure about what is expected of them.
- To respect people's feelings, if they do not want to be made into 'official' carers or if they do not want to be 'cared for', but just left in peace.
- To use common sense; avoid becoming fanatical or pompous; see the funny side.
- To encourage all pastors to pray together, meet for support, recognize each other's gifts, help forward each other's work, in short, to practise 'collaborative ministry'.

We have looked at what is being done in a wide variety of places and churches, all using different plans and methods. Some issues, however, come up again and again and are of concern to all churches, in their common desire for all people to know that they belong and are cherished — with the love that derives from God's love.

Story for discussion

5. Doreen

TOPICS
- Issues for Christians at work
- Support by the church
- Doing theology

Doreen is an ordinary Christian faced with a problem. She works as manager of a restaurant which is part of a large national chain. She has just been told by her Regional Manager that, owing to financial problems facing the whole chain, she must make one of her staff redundant — otherwise her restaurant may have to close. She has good relationships with all her staff and knows their personal stories — but one of them has to go.

First discussion

1   What issues does this situation raise?
2   How can Doreen think theologically (ask where God is) in this situation?
3   Can Doreen's membership of her church help her?

What she did

- She checked carefully on all the facts of the case, including the law relating to redundancy.
- She laid the problem before God in her prayers.
- She shared her anxiety with her fellowship group.
- She continued to think about it during the service on the following Sunday.
- She arranged to have a talk about it with a member of the pastoral team.

- Things began to come together in her mind and she could now see the situation more clearly and come to a decision.
- She talked over the decision with her senior staff members and they devised a plan of action together.

Second discussion

What do you think of the actions Doreen took?

WORKING TOGETHER

'Like good stewards of the manifold grace of God, serve one another with whatever gift each of you has received.' (1 Peter 4:10)

'The gifts he gave were that some would be apostles, some prophets, some evangelists, some pastors and teachers, to equip the saints for the work of ministry, for building up the body of Christ, until all of us come to the unity of the faith and of the knowledge of the Son of God, to maturity, to the measure of the full stature of Christ.' (Ephesians 4:11–13)

'Koinonia ... this mutual commitment is something deeper, more personal, and much more dynamic than our words "fellowship" or "communion" can ever convey. This mutual commitment, God to us, us to God, each of us to each other, is in stark contrast to the individualism which is where many of us have to start.' (Mark Birchall)[1]

It has frequently happened in our society that a particular need has been met because one person took action. The Rev. Chad Varah started the Samaritans to provide support for those in despair. Mrs Mary Sumner, when she saw young mothers in her husband's parish needing help with the moral and spiritual upbringing of their children, held meetings for them, which eventually grew into the worldwide Mothers' Union. Dr Cicely Saunders founded one of the first hospices for people suffering from terminal illness and so set in train the 'hospice movement'. The founding person's name is remembered with respect and often becomes a household word: Dr Barnado, Mother Teresa.

In New Testament times it was more usual for people to work in and with their communities. Doing things together – collaboration – came naturally to them. In the Christian community, to begin with, everyone shared in the key tasks. For example the distribution of food to those who were in need was not a piece of 'private enterprise', rather it was a communal activity (Acts 2:43–7). But as the community expanded this became inefficient and wasteful. It was necessary to assign different kinds of activity to different people – and we are told that everyone was satisfied with the arrangements that were made (Acts 6:1–7).

Perhaps it was not always as easy as the account in Acts makes it sound. As he looked back, Luke may have simplified the story. But the point remains: people of varying gifts were assigned particular jobs and they worked together harmoniously – at least for most of the time.

Circles of collaboration

Michael Hare-Duke, writing about recent developments in the Scottish Episcopal Church, commented: 'The pyramid of hierarchical authority is giving way to the circles of shared ministry.'[2] Today, if a diagram were to be drawn of the activities of a church that is trying to follow the New Testament pattern, it would look like a mesh of overlapping circles. Many of these 'church circles' would also overlap with other 'circles' representing activities in the community at large and the many different places where people work.

Every 'circle' – committee, working party, rota or group – can be a means of caring for and enabling its members. Belonging to any of these can be, in itself, an affirming experience. Usually the 'circles' are small enough for the members to get to know each other well and to look after each other; and for every member to play a useful part and feel valued. All this is not only true for the pastoral visiting team, but is equally valid for the coffee rota or the buildings committee.

A church that aims to manage its affairs through 'circles of collaboration' needs to develop two particular groups of skills: of leadership and of team working. Some of these skills are needed by ministers – those with oversight of church, parish or benefice. But they are also needed in each of the different 'circles', the groups, committees and activities that make up the life of a local church: in, for example, the staff group, eldership, church council, junior church leaders group, worship committee, church cleaning rota, outreach group, social events committee, house group, prayer group or baptism team. No single person can possess all these skills – but when ministry is truly collaborative each can depend upon the gifts of others to complement their own.

Leadership – in two churches

St Peter's Church publishes a monthly magazine, of which Richard was until lately the sole editor. He felt overburdened, because he could not find enough contributions and had to do most of the writing himself. He knew that the magazine had become dull and repetitive: little more than the 'Minister's Letter' and a report of the Women's Group meeting, with baptisms, marriages and funerals tacked on. But he felt he must continue because 'no one else wants to do it'.

Then Poppy, a lay reader, moved into the area and joined St Peter's. From her experience elsewhere she believed that an editorial group might work better. She suggested the idea to Richard and then approached two more people, Roy and

Heather. They both have busy lives, but she put it to them that the magazine is important – because it has a vital role in fostering a vision for the church and in binding people together as the body of Christ in their community. Both have agreed to give the magazine priority and to join the team, initially for half a year, after which there will be a review.

So now a group of four people meets on one evening a month to plan and produce the magazine – which is done by stapling photocopied pages together. While getting on with the practical work, they consider the content of the next issue. Roy is full of ideas: what about some reports of people's holidays, especially if they attended a different church while they were away? Shall we ask Mr S. to write an account of his job in the bank? What does he actually *do* there and what are the problems and the rewards of his work? Or P.C. Evans – *his* work must be tough – how does he cope? That Bible study at Ellen's house group last week seems to have caused controversy – could we have an account of that? Heather has a practical eye and has already suggested a quicker way to manage the collating and stapling. Richard, with his orderly mind, makes sure that they settle exactly who, during the next month, will be conducting this interview or writing that article. He has lost his anxious feelings and recovered his enthusiasm. Poppy has the knack of making them all feel that what they are doing is worthwhile. There is much laughter and drinking of coffee. The time spent together is enjoyable and productive.

At St Jude's, the Church Council has appointed a new 'Planning Group', with five members. This group has been asked to think ahead and come up with creative ideas for future events, such as away-days, competitions, concerts, outdoor worship or community projects. At its first meeting the group chose its 'officers'. Tony volunteered to act as secretary – to make notes at their meetings and distribute them. They decided to have a 'revolving chair': this means that they meet in each other's homes in turn, with the person in whose home the meeting is held acting as 'chair' for that occasion.

Tony, who likes to see church activities being efficiently managed, has some misgivings about this plan. He wonders whether Violet, for example, who is a quiet, thoughtful person, will be able to steer group meetings effectively. Alec is the opposite: he talks a lot, wants to get his own way and does not listen to others. The group is likely to bubble with ideas, but not necessarily to agree, so it may be difficult to get decisions made without having meetings that drag on for hours.

Tony has found out that a course is available entitled 'Taking a Lead', which starts next term at a nearby centre and he has persuaded the other four to join it with him. He has also drawn it to the attention of the whole congregation, in case there are others who might like to attend. This will help them to understand how a group works and how to run meetings efficiently.

• For a description of this course, see Chapter 12.

Qualities and skills of leadership

Both Poppy and Tony have been using a number of leadership skills. Poppy has a long-term vision for the magazine, which she has communicated to the others. She has supported and encouraged Richard. She found the right people to create a team, in which their different talents are being used. She guides the others gently so that the meetings are orderly and hard-working, as well as friendly and enjoyable.

Tony, too, has shown many leadership qualities. In a situation where no one had been nominated as an official leader he had the courage to take the initiative. He saw what needed to be done at once in order to get the group started: to get essential information circulated. He is taking initial responsibility for this himself, while suggesting a review after a few months. He has looked ahead and discerned both the possibilities for the group (lots of exciting new projects, efficient planning) and the likely difficulties (chaotic meetings, heated arguments, failure to decide anything). By arranging for the team to go on a training course, he has taken appropriate action.

In these two stories many of the main skills of leadership can be seen in action. They fall into three areas:

1   Communicating an inspiring vision.
2   Enabling people.
3   Ensuring that meetings are effective for their purpose.

Communicating vision

'Jesus came to Galilee, proclaiming the good news of God, and saying, "The time is fulfilled and the kingdom of God has come near..." ... And immediately ... they followed him' (Mark 1:14, 15, 18).

'If you don't know where you're going you'll end up somewhere else' (Rover Group handbook).[3]

Jesus proclaimed 'good news' – about God's purposes, power and love – with authority and conviction. The religious officials found his teaching too challenging and were soon trying to get rid of him, but all the ordinary people felt drawn to him. To inspire others with a vision of the Kingdom, leaders today need:

• to ask the Holy Spirit for guidance before starting any new enterprise;
• to discern how a particular project can help to build the Kingdom and strengthen the body of Christ in their local community;
• to keep the vision fresh and show people its relevance to their lives;
• to discern what action needs to be taken;
• to have the courage to take the initiative;
• to be willing to set an example by contributing their own time and effort;

- to be unwilling to take everything upon themselves for ever;
- to look ahead: for future possibilities – and problems;
- to accept that there is always more to learn.

Enabling people

Jesus always discerned the possibilities in people – he saw them as they could become. When Nathaniel was brought to Jesus by his friend Philip he was amazed by his insight. 'When Jesus saw Nathaniel coming toward him, he said of him, "Here is truly an Israelite in whom there is no deceit!" Nathaniel asked him, "Where did you get to know me?" Jesus answered, "I saw you under the fig tree before Philip called you." Nathaniel replied, "Rabbi, you are the Son of God...".' Nathaniel knew that Jesus had seen him in a special way (John 1:47–9).

Jesus chose a group of twelve to be his close friends; he called them to be with him, discerned their personalities, encouraged and nurtured, taught and trained them and gave them authority: 'And he appointed twelve ... to be with him and to be sent out to proclaim the message and to have authority to cast out demons' (Mark 3:14, 15). Especially in Mark's Gospel we often see Jesus dealing with their perplexed questions and explaining to them the underlying reasons for his teaching and practice. He sent them out to teach and heal – in twos, never alone (Mark 6:7).

At the very end of his earthly ministry he again gave authority to them. In spite of all their weaknesses and failures he delegated the continuing work to them and trusted them: 'Go therefore and make disciples of all nations, baptizing them ... and teaching them...' (Matthew 28:19, 20).

What kind of 'enabling'?

'The art of gardening is knowing about plants: knowing which ones are tall or short, which ones are striking in shape, at what time of year they produce their flowers and for how long, whether their colours are strong or delicate, which pests prey on them, whether they can stand up to frost or damp, whether they do best in full sun or in cool shade. They are all different and you have to get to know where to plant each kind and then how to care for them so that they grow strongly.'[4]

Enabling people is like gardening because people, like plants, vary widely. People who belong to their local churches vary in experience, in confidence and in their stage of spiritual growth. They therefore vary in the kind of 'enabling' they need.

On the one hand there is Reg, who is a church member. Reg has time on his hands but little self-confidence. He was once a skilled fitter, but has been unemployed for the past three years. His wife works part-time in the old people's home up the road. Reg spends some of his long days working on his allotment and likes to take his two children with him. In spite of this Reg often gets depressed, because he feels useless. Sometimes he even feels jealous of his wife's job.

However, he has recently been invited to join the garden committee of their church. He is shy at the meetings, but he sometimes plucks up courage to contribute. He has started seeing to small jobs in the churchyard – an untidy creeper on the wall or weeds in the path. The minister has also had the idea of asking Reg, since he obviously likes young people, to come along and help with the Junior Church's summer outing. So his days are beginning to fill up and his life feels more purposeful.

On the other hand there is Ron, who belongs to another church. Ron has confidence, but no spare time. He is Managing Director of a large firm. He chairs meetings every day, goes abroad frequently, negotiates difficult deals, manages public relations, supervises a large staff. He tries to run the business in an honest and humane manner, in accordance with Christ's teachings. If he has any time and energy over, he devotes them to his family. He gets to church when he can, but when he has been urged to stand for election to the church council he has had to say 'no' and feels guilty about it. What Ron needs from the church is assurance that everything he does in his work and with his family are authentic ways of serving Christ. Rather than expecting Ron to attend committee meetings, the church could benefit from his expertise by using him as a consultant on specific matters.

Then there is Jumila, who has little spare time, but she loves her church and has particular gifts to offer. She belongs to the Methodist church in a city suburb. She is married to Mustak and they have three almost-grown-up children. She does a demanding job as a social worker. She is a calm, perceptive person, whose Christian faith is the foundation of her whole existence. She loves belonging to the family of the church and longs to contribute to its life in some way. The church is desperate for people to help with the youth group and Jumila has several times been asked if she could spare an evening a week for this. But she has always refused because, in spite of having a family herself, she feels she is not cut out for organizing treasure hunts and table tennis tournaments. Also she is very tired when she gets home in the evening.

What she would like to do is join a prayer group, but no such group has existed in her church up to now. She is wondering if she should start one and has asked several Christian friends to pray for her as she makes plans. The 'enabling' that Jumila needs at the moment is encouragement to believe that she can go ahead and start to pray with one or two other people. The prayerful support she is receiving is beginning to give her confidence. She needs to know that the church is not nagging her to take on work that is inappropriate for her, but is behind her in this new venture to which she feels called.

In relating to people – and taking Jesus as our pattern – leaders today need:

- to help people to trust God and so to grow stronger and more confident;
- to look upon each person as someone infinitely valued by God;
- to understand people, especially by discerning the particular situation, strengths and gifts of each one, the stage reached, the potential for learning and growing, the particular kind of enabling needed: this discernment is itself a skill that grows with experience, aided by knowledge of human development;
- to give time to keeping in touch with people;
- to convey encouragement to people, so that their spirits are lifted;
- to communicate with people effectively, including being able to listen to them;
- to arrange for decisions to be taken by agreement and to be owned by everyone concerned;
- to ensure that people can work together in pairs and groups, rather than alone;
- to check out that each person has enough support, enough rest and enough family time;
- to give people hope;
- to like people and make them feel that you like them and that you enjoy being friends with them;
- to laugh and relax with people, so that they feel better about life.

Planning for better meetings: shared leadership, responsible membership

Jesus never attended any committees, working parties or discussion groups. He did constantly interact with people, however – he talked with his friends as they walked along the road, accepted hospitality in people's homes, entered into discussions with individuals, responded to those who came to see him, healed many sick people, taught crowds, clashed with authority figures.

He exercised every 'interpersonal skill' that was needed to get close to people, to comfort and encourage, inspire loyalty, widen horizons, stimulate and confront, challenge prejudice and 'speak the truth in love' (Ephesians 4:15). In the various 'circles' of a local church today – especially in all kinds of meetings, informal or formal – all leaders and members need to be sensitive and tactful, honest and forthright, self-effacing and peace-promoting: in fact to follow the example of Jesus.

The needs of a group: G - I - T

In any group there are three sets of needs, which can easily be remembered by the initials G - I - T.

First there is the need for maintenance of the **group**. This will include all the arrangements that are made to help people to relax and get to know each other, including the placing of chairs, the way people are introduced to each other, the provision of name badges (or not), the way the meeting begins and ends, the provision of refreshments; a 'design' that allows time for sharing and so for the building of trust – and many other factors.

Second, there are the needs of **individuals**. Each person needs to be made to feel welcome, to be physically comfortable, with chairs placed so that everyone can see and hear, the room not too hot or cold. Each person needs opportunities to contribute and to know that their contribution is appreciated.

Third, there are the needs of the **task** of the particular group. These will vary widely according to the group's purpose. A committee will put most of its effort into fulfilling its 'task' – getting through its agenda and making clear decisions. A house group, on the other hand, although it may have some tasks – perhaps of making progress in Bible study and agreeing on some future plans – will be mainly devoted to the needs of individuals and of the group's maintenance, as individuals are built up. The person with oversight – the 'leader', 'chair' or 'facilitator'

– will need to attend to all these needs, as is appropriate to the particular group. But it is helpful if every member understands these threefold needs and knows that each person has a particular and vital contribution to make in meeting them.

Dorothy belongs to her local Council for Voluntary Service, as the representative of a charity for which she works. The Council meetings are chaired with great efficiency, so that even with a long agenda the meetings are over in an hour. 'But,' says Dorothy, 'the chairman hurries us along so quickly that I can never get a word in and I sometimes wonder if there is any point in making the effort to attend. After the meetings are over, coffee is available, but people tend to disperse quickly and there is no chance of getting to know the other members or picking up tips from their experience.' Here the needs of the 'task' are apparently being met, but this Council would do its job even better, in the long term, if each member was encouraged to contribute, and better still if the members got to know each other and formed a closer group, which would enable useful 'networking' and mutual support to occur, imaginative ideas to be generated and plans to be made co-operatively.

Only when all three sets of needs are met does any group function with full effectiveness. If attention is given to the needs of the group and of the individuals within it, then the task will be carried out more successfully.

One church has worked out a 'format', given below, for the meetings of all the committees that run its various activities. This does not have to be rigidly adhered to, but it does provide a guiding framework and they find it works well.

An outline for meetings

1   Prayer and Bible reading, followed by some shared reflection on the Bible passage.
2   Recalling of the overall vision and purpose of the team within the Body of Christ.
3   Sharing of what has happened since last time and how each person is feeling now (see Chapter 12 for suggested exercises).

4   Agreement as to the specific agenda items for this meeting and the time to be spent on each. The agenda may include a review of ongoing projects and reports from other 'circles'.

5   Working through the agreed agenda – keeping to time as far as possible.

6   Summing up. Clarifying who is taking responsibility for the next step in each case.

7   Opportunity to raise any other matters of common concern.

8   Closing prayers.

GROUP PROCESS – WHAT IS GOING ON?

Everything that goes on in a group may be referred to as the 'process'. Some of this 'process' is obvious and visible: words are spoken, decisions are made. But underneath there is an invisible and complex criss-cross of thoughts and emotions, which frequently run counter to the obvious, visible part. This is the case whether the group is two people having a casual chat; ten at a formal committee; twenty at a party; or fifty at a conference. If we draw a diagram of a group of only six people, with lines drawn between them to show all the possible inter-actions that may be happening at the same time, the result looks like a spider's web with fifteen criss-crossing lines.

The members of any group should get into the habit of observing 'process', especially the less obvious part: first your own feelings and reactions; and then the clues given by others – their facial expressions, how they sit, their gestures and tone of voice, their reactions to each other. Being aware of 'process' will build understanding, especially if there are opportunities for bringing feelings out into the open. When people are helped by the actions or words of others, it strengthens the whole group to know about it. When people feel frustrated, misunderstood or overlooked, tension will be defused if these feelings are openly shared. When people understand each other, they will be more ready to be honest and to trust each other. Decisions will be 'owned' by everyone. All will be better motivated and energized for action.

To make all kinds of meetings human and effective, leaders today need:

- to be ready to learn how groups work – including social gatherings, business meetings, study sessions and meetings for prayer and fellowship;
- to encourage and enable each member to contribute in different ways; to appreciate and use each contribution;
- to know how to handle difficult situations – such as when one person dominates a group;
- to develop the special skills – whether as chairperson or member – of getting business done, decisions made, conflicts resolved and compromises reached;
- to have a clear 'agenda', but be ready to depart from it if the Spirit leads the group in another direction;
- when 'in the chair', to be able to sum up, clarify decisions, move the group on to the next item;
- to keep to time, so that people are not worried about being late for fetching children from school or for another appointment (or for their bedtime);
- to be 'tea makers' and 'room arrangers' – to ensure that the setting helps people to get on well together and that meetings are enjoyable.

Teamworking

Secular manuals on management usually have a section about 'assembling' or 'picking' your team. But in a voluntary organization like the church it is rarely possible for a team to be chosen. More often it is a case of appealing for volunteers and being thankful when a few come forward. Or perhaps the people are already there – they are already doing certain jobs – but the need has now arisen for them to start working together as a team. What do we mean by a 'team'? What does an effective team look like? And how can an effective team be built out of a random group of disparate personalities?

A rowing 'eight' has to be strong on teamwork. All the members have to pull precisely together, in order to achieve their common aim – which is to beat all the other eights competing in the regatta and so to win glory for their school, their club or their country. The various teams or 'circles' of a local church are also working together towards a common aim: not to win glory, but to serve people – and to do it not by competing but by co-operating.

A newspaper photograph carries the caption: 'A soldier demonstrates the art of teamwork'.[5] Two soldiers are shown scaling a high brick wall. Soldier Number One stands with his boots on one shoulder of Soldier Number Two. Number Two supports the feet of Number One with his hands, but his face is turned aside, its expression contorted into a mixture of fear and pain. Entrusting their safety to each other takes courage – and even a readiness to suffer: but together they can reach heights that separately they could not achieve.

The Rover Group of car manufacturers involves its workforce in a programme of Total Quality Improvement, of which one of the key themes is 'Teamwork'. The company's handbook asserts:

By working in teams we can:
– achieve things individuals cannot
– make the best use of our skills
– make better decisions
– get more enjoyment from our work

In order to work together in teams Rover's key advice is: 'Always try to see things from other people's point of view before disagreeing with them!'[6]

Raymond Blanc, chef-proprietor of Le Manoir Aux Quat' Saisons Hotel in Oxfordshire, attributes his success to teamwork:

'People do not work for me, they work with me, as part of a team, and they have to be highly involved.' Every month seven or eight staff from different departments discuss their work while they eat in the dining room: 'if a chef meets a washer-up, a waiter, a chambermaid, an accountant and a gardener it helps teamwork. They realise that other people are important too'.[7]

Hugh is a minister in a large suburban church. He became disillusioned when he tried giving responsibility to a lay member of his congregation. 'I delegated the over-sight of pastoral care to Maggie, a member of the congregation who is a very efficient housewife. It ran smoothly for several years. Then she suddenly told me that her husband's financial situation made it necessary for her to get a paid job, so she couldn't any longer run the church's "care scheme". I felt completely let down, especially as I knew that various needy people would suffer, at least for a time. I am not sure now that it makes sense to delegate.' What went wrong here? Why did Maggie's situation reach crisis point before Hugh had any idea that she and her husband were in difficulties?

Hugh wrote later: 'I realize now that I was working alone and that this was my mistake. I took the decision alone to delegate the organizing of pastoral care to someone else. I did not keep in touch with what Maggie was doing or how she was coping. She had formed a team of pastoral visitors to care for people in the parish, but was not cared for herself. All her arrangements depended on her own day-to-day organizing and checking, so when she gave up I could not be sure that the pastoral team would carry on.'

Hugh had discovered that delegation, though it has its place, is not the same as working together with others. Through his own practice he had given Maggie a model of working and taking decisions alone, which she in her turn had adopted. This solitary way of working meant that in the end the whole 'set-up' collapsed and many people were hurt. Maggie felt anxious and guilty. Hugh felt bewildered and disillusioned. Some people who needed visiting were bereft of care for a while. However, with the help of a lay person experienced in both management and the ways of churches, Hugh has now done some careful reflection on all this, and in future will be making a point of drawing in others and working together.

Janie is an assistant minister in a rural situation, where several churches are overseen by a ministerial team. When she first joined it, the team consisted entirely of clergy. Team meetings were brief and confined to necessary business ('What will be the most convenient picking-up point for the church outing?' 'Who will get the posters printed for the harvest supper?'). There was no encouragement to them to be open with each other, nor did they share problems or resources.

Recently everything has been transformed by the arrival of a new Team Rector, Donald, who believes in collaborative ministry. He requested that a longer time be set aside for weekly team meetings. He began sharing some of his own problems with the others, which led to a more honest climate, in which it became possible for all the ministers to speak about their feelings – their joys and their disappointments – and to offer each other support, advice and practical help. Donald also invited the two Lay Readers in the benefice to join the team and attend the meetings whenever they could. Ruby works in public relations, Alistair has a senior position in a firm that produces computer software. They have brought a wider perspective to the discussions – as well as a measure of impatience! They are ready to give up time to the meetings, but are not prepared to sit through lengthy rambling chat. In the business world they are used to clarity of overall purpose, a well-prepared agenda for meetings, a co-operative attitude on the part of all staff, a readiness to take decisions and a plan of action to carry them out.

Guidelines for teamworking

From all these examples, a picture of an effective team emerges:

- At least the facilitator of the team – but preferably every member – is committed to the ideal of working together – of co-operating rather than competing, of sharing rather than shouldering the whole burden oneself, of being open rather than defensive. An attitude of goodwill – of trying always to see other points of view – is cultivated.
- There is clarity – and agreement – on broad aims, immediate objectives, individual roles.
- Time is given for hidden agendas and feelings to be brought into the open, so that trust is built up.
- Disagreements, when they occur (as they will), are not seen as the end of the world, but are faced calmly and seen as opportunities for growing. Understanding of human personality, of group dynamics and of techniques for conflict resolution will help, as will a sense of humour and a willingness to 'learn as we go along'.
- Trouble is taken to look outwards, as well as inwards at the group's own agenda and practice, by keeping in touch with other circles and networks. This may be done, for example, by giving and hearing reports, by joint meetings and events.
- Reviews of the group's work, with stringent evaluation, are carried out regularly. Feedback is requested: for example through questionnaires or a church conference. Time is given for reflection on all these so that future practice can be improved.

A minister sums it up: 'The image I like best is of a jazz group. There is a common theme. There is respect for each musician's skill and creative flair. Each performer is glad to move from solo improvisation to support and back again. There is acute listening to each other as well as room for fierce dispute as both these increase creativity. Sometimes there is a leader overall, but there does not have to be. You create the music as you go along – and that seems more like working out God's call in our own settings.'[8]

Story for discussion

6. Duncan

TOPICS
- Support by the 'church family'
- Can ministers help?
- Giving advice
- Responding to people's needs

'When the firm by whom I had been employed for the past fourteen years was taken over last year I was offered redundancy or relocation. After many hours of discussion with my wife I opted for relocation. We put our house on the market, and began looking for a house in the new place. The children, too, showed understanding about having to leave their friends and began to be enthusiastic about the move.

'Then the purchasing company decided we were to be made redundant after all and we had to explain to the children that the move was off. Yet again I was aware of the support of the whole family. People at church, after the usual commiseration and telling me that it happened to a lot of people and that "X" in the congregation was still looking for work after five years, appeared to rub their hands with glee. It was almost, "Yippee, here comes the unpaid 'lay pastoral assistant' we need!"

'I actually found another job within a short space of time but the church has still not adjusted to the idea that I am not available for meetings every night of the week. I think it is an example of what Pastoral Care should and should not be. There was the quiet support from my wife, enabling me to get through a form of bereavement and rejection, to talk through my feelings and thereby to sort out for myself the various problems and see more clearly the way ahead.

'But from the church came the example of what Pastoral Care should not be: "what you should do is..." and "I know a person who..." — and rushing to tell you what you could do to fill your time. All their "similar experiences" were interesting and shared with the best intentions, but were unhelpful to me at the time.'

Responses to this story from one group

• People need support from outside the family as well as within it.

• Sometimes 'the church' sees a human problem selfishly and narrowly: 'He's been made redundant, perhaps he could help with the youth group?'

• It is too easy to make assumptions about what someone else needs.

• Advice can be either helpful or unhelpful. Could we think of some guidelines?

• Churches talk about 'caring', but often the church as a community does not seem to be really committed to it.

• When someone suffers any severe loss they need to be drawn back sensitively into the community of the church.

• People need to feel that you are interested in them individually.

Discussion

1   What would be the best ways for people in the church to respond, when a member of the congregation is made redundant — or suffers any other severe loss?

2   What kind of caring support should people receive from the church?

3   How can ministers help this to happen?

6

VISITING OUR NEIGHBOURS

'I'm glad you've come'

'Paul said to Barnabas, "Come let us return and visit the believers in every city where we proclaimed the word of the Lord and see how they are doing".' (Acts 15:36)

'Lots of people popped in and I felt surrounded by love.'

'On the days I don't have meals-on-wheels I can go all day without seeing a soul – and sometimes I do long to hear the door-bell ring.'

Well-meant notice in a church magazine: 'The Vicar is always glad to hear of anyone who is sick.'

The heart of ministry

As we have seen, many people think of 'visiting' as a clergy role. The bell rings: *'Help, it's the minister!'* There may be a minor panic, but really the family are pleased. The minister has come, not for any special reason, not in order to find more people to do church cleaning or grass cutting or typing, but just for themselves. The minister has simply come to see them, accept a cup of tea, have a chat about nothing in particular, make them feel they are interesting and likeable.

One minister who believes that visiting is at the heart of his calling declares: 'A random appearance of a vicar opens up all sorts of opportunities.'[1] But other ministers take the view that routine visiting is no longer practically possible. A minister who looks after four widely separated country churches describes how his working week gets filled up – and the importance he also gives to spending time with his wife and family. He concludes: 'Of course the traditional stereotype of a personal, pastoral, caring vicar, endlessly visiting, is the ideal; but for most of us it is cruelly unrealistic.'[2]

Keith, whose ministry is in the Midlands, in what was originally a village but then expanded to become an industrial town, takes a positive view: 'It's a matter of how I weigh up my priorities. I am involved in a great many community projects: for that and other reasons, I don't do "routine visiting". I haven't time for popping in for a cup of tea. I encourage people to arrange to see me if they really want to and then I will give them a full hour of "quality time".' Even though he does not visit, he seems to know everyone. As he walks along the street he dispenses cheerful greetings: 'Hallo, Jenny! How are you? Are you OK? Good! Take care, God bless ... Hallo, Joan, how's Dave? ... Morning, Peter, I heard you'd had flu, look after yourself now!'

Keith's assessment of priorities is shared by many ministers today. But lay people may have more time for visiting – and in most situations are just as suitable, although there are probably some people who will never fully accept the ministry of anyone who is not ordained: 'It's just not the same if it isn't the minister!'

Neither Jesus nor the disciples appear to have visited individuals 'pastorally' in the sense we understand now. Presumably, at that time and in that culture it would not have been an appropriate or effective way of caring for people. But Jesus often entered and stayed in people's homes. Indeed, it appears that he never had a home of his own (apart from that of his family), so he depended greatly upon being given hospitality in households such as that of Mary, Martha and Lazarus. When he sent his disciples out with the Good News he urged them to live in dependence on the hospitality of others. They were to be with other people so that they could show them God's love. And they were to be willing to receive as well as to give.

Why visit?

It is not *always* the best way — but those who undertake pastoral care find that there are times when there is value in 'visiting': in calling on individuals to talk to them personally, in their homes or in hospital. It is still the best way to express love, bring comfort, build trust. And in our fractured, frenetic society, most people are glad to be visited.

A visit can be informal and spontaneous — the unannounced 'popping in' that is a natural and frequent occurrence among neighbours. Or it can be more formal, with the time arranged beforehand. It may be a 'one off', to deliver an invitation to a coffee morning to raise funds for children in Romania, perhaps, or to Lenten lunches for Christian Aid. It may be one of a series of regular calls on Bill who has become housebound, on Elsie who has no family members living near, or on Tunku and Norelle who have just had their first baby. Or it may be to give a welcome to someone who has just moved into your street.

A visit may be prompted by a sudden crisis: Christine has broken her ankle, her leg has been put into plaster and she cannot care for her toddler and baby while her husband is at work ... so Janet goes to see her to talk over with her a plan for a rota of people to come in and help. Or visiting may be for the purpose of staying alongside someone who is in deep distress: Geoff's wife, Jean, died of cancer at a tragically young age; he was racked by anger and frustration and unbearable grief; so

Tom, who had undertaken some training in bereavement support, went to see him regularly for many months.

On the other hand, a visit may be just a visit, simply for the purpose of human contact. Many visits take place as a result of natural kindness and friendliness. Generally people know what to say and what help to offer – guided by their instincts and by their past experience. But it also happens, particularly where there has been a death, whether sudden or expected, that people do *not* know what to say and therefore they try to avoid the bereaved relatives. It is not easy to be as articulate as the double-glazing salesman or political canvasser, who knows exactly what he wants to say.

In between visits there's the telephone ('It's good to talk', as British Telecom assures its UK customers) or one can send a card – both useful ways of keeping in touch.

Guidelines for good practice in visiting

'Whatever house you enter, first say "Peace to this house!"' (Luke 10:5)

'It's kind of her to come, but sometimes I wish she wouldn't. I can't follow all her talk and I feel exhausted by the time she goes.' (Church member)

'Go as a friend, not to patronize. And remember that an older – or ill – person is the same person as before.' (Experienced member of a pastoral team)

Training can help
In one area, a three-session course, entitled 'What do I say?', was arranged for church members who wanted to become more effective visitors.

Part 1 offered suggestions for 'How to be a good visitor'.

Part 2 included practice in 'Listening Skills'.

Part 3 was particularly related to 'Bereavement Listening'.

The course was quickly oversubscribed: clearly people felt that, if they were to give effective support to those in distress, they needed guidance – and help in developing their skills.

Guidance can be given by means of a structured course – such as the one described above – or through discussion at 'support meetings'. Here are some of the questions that are likely to be raised.

IF I VISIT AS A REPRESENTATIVE OF THE CHURCH, IS IT ANY DIFFERENT FROM VISITING AS A CONCERNED NEIGHBOUR?

Naturally the two roles overlap. But as a member of the church, you have something distinctive to offer (discussed more fully in Chapter 1). You bring to the relationship your awareness of the predicament of all human beings before God, of God's judgement and God's mercy, and of the grace we can receive through Jesus Christ, to strengthen us in coping with all the complicated problems of living. You will have the sense not to 'go on' about this, but, as you try to build friendship and trust, your approach will be coloured by your belief in each person's eternal destiny.

IS IT IMPORTANT TO ESTABLISH MY AUTHORITY AS A VISITOR? WHAT IS THE BEST WAY OF DOING THIS?

Yes, as it will help to ensure that, whether you are clergy or lay, you will be well received. Some churches give their pastoral visitors a distinctive badge to identify themselves – which is important today when strangers may be suspect. When the door is opened you can say: 'I belong to the church's pastoral team', or 'The minister asked me to call'.

IS IT ALWAYS BEST TO FIX A TIME IN ADVANCE, BY RINGING UP FIRST — IF THEY ARE ON THE PHONE — OR SENDING A NOTE?

This is almost always the best way, if only out of consideration to the person's spouse or 'carer'. If they live alone and do not know you, they will naturally be unwilling to open the door to an unexpected stranger. If the person is in hospital you may need to check visiting hours or make arrangements with the person in charge of the ward.

IS IT NECESSARY TO GET THE PERSON'S CONSENT BEFORE VISITING?

This is always a good idea, but it can be done quite informally. You can simply ask: 'Can I come and see you?' or 'May I come in?' Be alert to pick up any hesitancy. Be available, but sensitive about not pushing in when it is not welcome or not convenient.

WHAT PREPARATION FOR A VISIT SHOULD I DO?

It is helpful to give some thought to a visit beforehand. Clarify in your own mind what the main purpose of the visit will be. For example, will it be mainly to give encouragement? Or to see if you can help in any practical way? Or to give reassurance — if you think they may be anxious? But you must also be flexible enough to respond to the person's needs when you are there.

HOW SHOULD I PRAY BEFORE A VISIT?

In all your thinking about the visit beforehand remember that, if you consciously tune in to God's love and ask the Holy Spirit to guide you, God's love will flow between you and the person you are going to visit. Pray while you are having a sandwich before you go or as you drive or walk to the person's home. Afterwards, as you go home, commit the visit to be used according to God's loving purposes; ask for God's healing touch on both of you; pray to be shown the next step; give thanks for the friendship, appreciation, or satisfaction that you have received yourself from the visit.

SHOULD I FIX A TIME LIMIT IN MY OWN MIND?

This is a good idea, as it is better to stay too short than too long a time. People often find that 'being visited' makes them tired. So it may be best to keep your visit short and go again on another day. But you must look out for clues and respond to the person's needs as you perceive them at the time.

IS THERE A 'PATTERN' THAT A VISIT SHOULD ALWAYS FOLLOW?

The following pattern has been found to work well — but again you need to be flexible:

- Opening: comment on the cat, the budgie or the weather — something non-personal.
- Central sharing: focus on the other person and on your reason for coming.
- Closing summary: make an agreement about when you will come again.
- Finally, before you go: back to 'the budgie'.

SHOULD I PRAY WITH THE PERSON I AM VISITING?

Only you can judge whether to suggest prayer. Many people would not think of this for themselves or would be afraid to ask, but are pleased if you suggest it. If you decide to take a chance, be alert to pick up whether praying together is a familiar or a new experience, causes embarrassment or is appreciated.

SHOULD I LEAVE SOMETHING BEHIND: A SMALL GIFT OR PERHAPS SOME CHRISTIAN LITERATURE OR THE PARISH MAGAZINE?

This is a good idea — but think carefully what to leave. A frivolous women's magazine might be just the thing for a university teacher when she is feeling ill; a modern novel full of romantic passion might be relished by an elderly single lady — but either would be risky. Try to find something appropriate for the particular person – and do not feel you have to do it every time.

WHAT RECORDS SHOULD I KEEP? I HAVE A BAD MEMORY.

Everything that happens or is said during a visit must be treated as confidential. Have a small notebook, in which you record only facts, such as the date and timing of the visit and names of family members. You could add cryptic notes to jog your memory when you go next time. Only the basic facts should be given to a minister or pastoral team leader. If you think there is something more that ought to be passed on to a minister, relative or doctor, you must get the person's permission first. If this is not forthcoming and you still feel it is necessary to speak to someone else, you should make quite clear to the person what you intend to do.

SHOULD I INVITE THE PERSON I AM VISITING TO COME TO MY HOME?

Only you can decide whether this would be helpful and appropriate. Hospitality certainly contributes to ministry and we should encourage it in the churches. On the other hand, consider whether inviting someone to your home might create expectations of a closer relationship than you can offer – or whether you might be asking too much of your family.

Ministry to people who are ill

People seem to visit most often because someone is ill: either with a short-term illness, such as a bad cold, flu or bronchitis, or with a chronic or terminal illness, such as cancer or AIDS, or from mental illness.

What it feels like to be ill

A group in one local church had some discussions on pastoral care. They began by recalling, from their own experience, what it feels like to be ill:

Felt terrible

Had physical symptoms

Lost confidence

It touched my pride

Felt frustrated

Felt intolerant

Was not sure if I ought to be ill

Had conflicting feelings

Felt ashamed

Felt uneasy, something wrong

Felt worried

Felt frightened

Felt guilty

Felt I'd failed

Felt completely cut off

Felt 'low'

Couldn't do anything

Felt undignified

Felt powerless and helpless

Got angry and bad-tempered

Was not sure if I was really ill

Wanted it to go away

Was overwhelmed by the pain

Wanted people to go away

Wanted to rest

Wanted oblivion

Wanted to hide

Felt exhausted

Felt dependent on God

They agreed that being ill:

• gives people a certain status;
• sometimes carries a stigma — a diagnosis and 'label' can separate an ill person from other people and from normal life;
• carries some rights, such as:
  – not to work;
  – to receive medical care;
  – to receive care from others;
• carries some obligations, such as:
  – to get well again as soon as possible;
  – to receive and take advice;
  – to be pleased to be visited.

People's needs when they are ill

Needs differ widely according to circumstances and individual temperament, so that those who visit should be alert to pick up clues. Most ill people have all or some of the following needs:

- for encouragement;
- for hope;
- for reassurance that they are not a nuisance, a fraud, wicked, peculiar, going mad, or all alone;
- for news;
- for various kinds of practical help;
- for appropriate suggestions for other kinds of available help.

Resources for those who visit the sick

Some of the following are natural resources, others need to be practised or acquired.

- Words
- Imagination and empathy
- Our own experience
- Prayer
- Thinking
- Faith and confidence in God's love
- Self-understanding:
  − to make a realistic assessment of what care we can offer, in the light of our circumstances and our particular gifts
  − to become aware of our motives and the rewards we expect
- Knowledge about psychology and theories of human development
- Friendship
- Relationship with God
- Appropriate action
- Knowledge of other sources of help, including practical help

Good practice in visiting people who are ill

We should ask: 'What does this particular person need and want at this time?' and respond accordingly. The person may just need to know you are there, without many words. You can give assurance that this is all right, simply sitting there quietly, not feeling you have to fill every silence – and avoiding staying too long.

The person may want to talk, may need a good listener, especially if they are on their own a great deal. Or they may prefer to listen – to some news of their church, perhaps, or of the outside world, something funny to cheer them up, or something that is read aloud.

Body language needs care: it is important to look attentive and not keep glancing at the clock; be ready to hold their hand or put an arm round them, but only if they seem clearly to want it and if it is appropriate. We can show them that it is all right to cry – or be angry or to voice their fears, frustration, guilt or depression; offer 'a shoulder to cry on' and have some tissues ready (but not too obviously) in case of need.

'Spiritual help' can be offered in the following ways, but try to get a 'feel' for how any of these suggestions would be received. If you cannot be sure, try it anyway, but be careful not to impose anything that does not seem acceptable.

- Give words of assurance of God's love.
- Speak personally about what has been helpful to you: 'When I have been ill I have found it a relief to hold on to the promise that God cares about me.'
- Ask if they would like to pray or read the Bible now.
- Promise to remember them in your own prayers.
- Suggest intercession for them by name in a church service and by the prayer group.
- Suggest that a minister or authorized lay person brings them extended Communion.
- Leave behind a prayer card or booklet.

Ministry to people who are facing old age, terminal illness and approaching death

'Look not back in anger, nor ahead in fear, but around in awareness.' *(James Thurber)*

> *Even such is Time, which takes in trust*
> *Our youth, our joys, and all we have,*
> *And pays us but with age and dust,*
> *Who in the dark and silent grave*
> *When we have wandered all our ways*
> *Shuts up the story of our days,*
> *And from which earth, and grave, and dust*
> *The Lord shall raise me up, I trust.*
> *(Sir Walter Raleigh)*[3]

Many people now spend one-third of their lives in retirement, often feeling they are 'redundant'. Many, as they get older, dislike the process and try to run away from it. They need sympathy and support, for ageing is a kind of death – a saying goodbye.

What do we feel when as adults we lose our parents, or a sibling? When for the first time we experience the death of a friend of our own age? We need to face and come to terms with our own approaching old age and our own death before we can support those who already feel useless, are frightened of old age, or know they are going to die soon.

What to expect when we visit

These are some typical reactions to the approach of death:

- Denial: 'No, not me, it can't be true.' Sometimes there is a complete refusal to face it, and no preparations are made. For example, no will is made. For some Christians it is belief in 'eternal life' that gives them an excuse for 'denial' of the reality of death.

- Anger, bitterness and a sense of isolation.
- An urge to blame someone: the doctors, God, people in the church, family members, or 'luckier' people.
- Bargaining with God in prayer.
- Depression. This may be either *reactive*: a reaction to what is happening, for example weight loss or pain – or *preparatory*: having to face the future loss of loved ones and loved things.
- Some people face death serenely and positively – nowadays often helped by efficient pain control – putting our fears to shame.

A visitor may well feel disturbed by these reactions, but it is best not to get involved in theological discussions at this point; instead just try to understand feelings, to hear what is behind the words. Sometimes a situation can be eased by taking simple practical steps, such as finding a hairdresser who will come to the house.

The family
Few people age or die entirely on their own. Family members are likely to be distressed and to need comfort and a listening ear themselves. But help must be offered with sensitivity: if the doorbell and the phone ring constantly, a spouse or other carer may long for these people who want to help to leave them alone instead. When chatting to carers or family members we need to be particularly watchful of ourselves, so that we do not impose unasked-for advice upon them – or egoistic accounts of our own past sufferings: 'I felt just the same...'

Possible reactions by family members include:

- Difficulty in adjusting to a completely new and deeply worrying situation. 'How will I be able to manage?'
- Denial, which may take the form of collusive silence.
- Shopping around for other cures or treatment – which may make the ill person feel even more anxious.

- Anger, resentment, impatience.
- Possessiveness – inability to allow the ill person to start the necessary process of 'letting go'.
- Guilt – about decisions they have made, such as allowing their relative to go – or not go – into hospital.
- Bewilderment and distress, especially if the sick person suffers personality changes or becomes increasingly helpless.

Support for those who are dying

We need to distinguish in our minds between those who:

- Know they are dying.
- Share this knowledge with family and friends.
- Do not appear to know.
- Do not know.

It may not be possible to tell how much the person we are visiting knows, but in any case we should support them in withdrawing rather than clinging on; in accepting the situation and developing some detachment; in living for the day; in enjoying simple things at this moment. These are not the same as 'denial'.

Positive acceptance can often be encouraged more easily by someone who is not a relative. You, as a visitor from outside the household, *may* be the only person they can trust and with whom they can be completely honest, so be a bit bold with questioning – it is worth the risk. Ask how they feel, how much time they think they have left, what their main anxieties are, whether there are any things they specially want to say or do. They will want you to be honest and *not afraid* to accept their situation.

Often the best reassurance can be given by touch, gesture, facial expression, listening – or by just staying there – rather than by words.

Questions for a training group to consider

1 What can we find in the Bible to guide us in supporting those who are ill or dying?
2 What do we mean by 'ministry to the sick'?
3 What are our motives in wanting to take part in this ministry? What 'rewards' do we expect?
4 What does illness mean in people's lives? What effect does it have on them?
5 When we ourselves are ill, how do we feel about accepting 'ministry' from others?

Who else?

Are there other groups of people, besides those who are ill, who feel isolated and might welcome a call? One might consider parents of young children, especially mothers; parents of children with physical handicaps or learning difficulties; people who are unemployed, especially anyone who has recently been made redundant; those who are single or have no children, who are often overlooked. And what about people who are not in any particular need, but might still appreciate your friendship? These, and others, may quickly say, when they see you on the doorstep: 'I'm glad you've come!'

Story for discussion

7. Viv, Len, Toni and Gillian

TOPICS
- Support by the church
- Listening
- Family relationships
- Parents and teenagers

Len and Viv are in their late forties. They had a turbulent marriage: both had affairs at various times. Now they are separated, though they still live near each other. Viv has a 16-year-old daughter, Toni, by a previous marriage — but Len adopted her. Viv works in the local branch of an estate agent, but she is worried that she may soon be made redundant — which has made her touchy and irritable lately.

Last summer Toni left school and got herself a job in a local shop — very much against Viv's wishes. They had several bitter rows. Then Toni left home, without telling anyone where she was going. Since then Len has managed to find out that Toni has moved in with her boyfriend — but they do not know her address. Viv feels distraught. She is worried about Toni's safety; she feels guilty; she thinks she has been a failure as a parent; she feels angry; she finds that her life is now quite empty.

Last Sunday she went to church, for the first time for some months. After the service, she was approached by Gillian, a friend who has known the family for a long time and is aware of the situation. Gillian picked up that Viv was unhappy and suggested dropping in one evening during the week for a talk.

Use the story as a role-play exercise

First read the story. Then divide into groups of three and decide who will take the roles of Viv, of Gillian, and of an 'observer'. Take a few minutes to consider the situation. Then 'Viv' and 'Gillian' talk together, with the 'observer' listening. While they are talking, the observer should notice their reactions to each other and especially their body language. After ten minutes the observer asks them to round off their conversations and then come out of role. Remain in the small groups and discuss the experience.

Discussion

1   Did Viv feel Gillian had been of any help and in what way? Did Gillian pick up her real feelings?
2   Did Gillian feel she could give any help to Viv, now or in the future? In what way?
3   Did the observer notice anything about what happened between them?
4   Is any help available from the church in this situation?

7

PREPARING FOR MARRIAGE

'We want to be married in church.'

'It was so good to have just three evenings to take a break from talking about the wedding to dicuss what we were really interested in — being married.'

'All we had was a five-minute chat — because we were regular church-goers an assumption was made — "I don't need to tell you about the Christian side of things." '

'One hour with the vicar, answering embarrassing questions.'

'I can only remember the minister giving me two words of advice, but I have often recalled them and found them helpful: "be patient".'

Today there is still a big demand for marriage in church. People want this for many different reasons, from the desire to make a social splash to the sense that a religious ceremony will help the relationship to endure. The request for a church wedding usually comes initially to one of the clergy — who then have an opportunity — and an important responsibility — to help the couple to 'prepare', both for the 'wedding' and for 'marriage'. There is growing public recognition that careful 'preparation' before marriage does help couples to build enduring marriages.

The charity One plus One has conducted research which shows that 'the odds of staying together can be dramatically improved if couples receive training before marriage in how to handle conflict.'[1]

A senior lawyer has set up a 'task force' at national level in Britain which aims to generate new ways of helping married couples to stay together. He is keen to persuade couples to seek advice before they marry: 'I would regard it as a practical matter to prepare people for marriage and the responsibilities of marriage.'[2]

Cardinal Basil Hume asserts: 'One urgent need is for better marriage preparation to be available to all ... what is needed is more investment in preparing for marriage...'[3]

Unfortunately, however, marriage preparation is normally only offered to couples who want to be married in church – though there seems no reason why courses run by secular counselling agencies should not be available for those who marry in a register office or elsewhere.

This chapter includes:

- Results of a small survey on marriage preparation
- Providing marriage preparation in the local church
- Outline of a sample course
- Suggestions for training leaders

A small survey

A group of men and women who belonged to an ordination training course attended a weekend seminar on the theme of marriage preparation. They were asked to inquire beforehand about how it was done in their own church or in any other churches they had contact with; if they themselves were married, to describe what preparation they had received; and to question one or two married friends about their experience.

'What marriage preparation did you receive yourself?'
Those who replied to this question had all received some preparation for the wedding, which had usually involved going through the service, with the emphasis on what would happen and when; contact with the organist about hymns; and a rehearsal. For many of them no preparation at all had been offered for marriage. Perhaps this was because, as church-goers or as ordinands, they were assumed to know enough already. Possibly the particular minister they had approached was one of the few who do not believe in the usefulness of formal marriage preparation. In some cases preparation had been minimal or unsatisfactory. But more often there had been talks with a minister, which in general had been appreciated as helpful.

- One couple had talked with the vicar and his wife together, 'about expectations of marriage and in a gentle, coded way about the non-stereotypical experience of sex that most couples have.'
- One couple who were at the time living far apart from each other had received teaching separately from their respective ministers.
- Several couples had unofficially approached married friends for advice, both clergy and lay: 'We spoke to a Congregational Minister and his wife (good friends of my wife) about the level of commitment involved and about their own experiences, especially the likelihood of "downs" in the early years.'
- Only one couple had been offered 'preparation' sessions in which help was also given by anyone other than the minister they had approached initially: 'We had four sessions with a team: the Rector and some lay people.'

What happens in churches you know?

Members of this group also, however, referred to churches they knew about in which quite extended preparation was available – two or three meetings – usually conducted by a minister, sometimes in partnership with their spouse.

- 'In our group of parishes it is done by the vicar and his wife for several couples together over one week-end, so they get to know the couples in depth. But it seems a pity that the couples see only one model of marriage.'
- Some of the descriptions were very positive: 'The minister sees his function as essentially pastoral and affirmative. He takes great care over the Order of Service, explaining the meaning of the symbols – as a lead into the meaning of Christian marriage. He makes a point of praying for them – and with them.'
- 'Our minister first clarifies why they want to be married and why in church. Then he covers trust, communication, sexual matters – not making any assumptions about whether they are or are not already experienced sexually, and not assuming that if they are experienced they have no difficulties.'
- 'Three individual meetings with a minister, plus one evening for several couples together – a structured enjoyable evening. Questionnaires used: know yourself, clarify your expectations. Encouragement to write down your commitment on various aspects of married life, such as deciding to spend at least one evening together each week. But not all couples manage to attend all this – or see the need for it. They are not allowed to come on their own – it must be as a couple.' (*Note*: most ministers recognize the possible difficulties here and do not insist on couples attending together.)
- There were several mentions of courses to which lay people had contributed: 'At our church there are three meetings: with a minister, a bank manager and a nurse.'

- 'In a church I know there is an initial meeting with a minister, at which the date and time of the wedding are fixed and an opportunity is offered of attending a course run by a lay couple in their home. Various videos, booklets and questionnaires are used as aids, to clarify expectations and give specifically Christian teaching.'

Summary
The survey revealed a wide variety of practices. Some people felt they had been well provided for by the church, while others wished they had received more help, especially with both practical matters and 'interpersonal skills'.

Marriage preparation in the local church

If you – and your church – are considering providing some form of marriage preparation for the first time, or if you want to review what is done at present, the next steps to take are to decide on your aims and objectives, the best arrangements for achieving them and the design of any course you may decide to offer.

Work out your aims
Broad aims might be to help a couple:

- to think out for themselves the deeper meaning of marriage, and especially of Christian marriage;
- to think out and compare their expectations of marriage;
- to find and start using some 'tools' for communication;
- to consider their future roles within their marriage;
- to identify practical matters that need to be discussed beforehand, and note what advice is available.

There are also many possible specific objectives, including:

- to talk about a number of issues in relation to money;
- to provide an opportunity for the sexual side of marriage to be discussed;
- to give teaching on the significance of being married in church: the Christian view of the marriage commitment;
- to help couples to clarify and compare their expectations and increase their self-understanding;
- to give couples practice in communicating well, resolving quarrels and giving each other encouragement;
- to offer models of marriage, by looking at the experiences of some married people;
- to demonstrate how prayer helps and to show couples how, if they have not done so already, they might pray together;
- to consider the importance of trusting each other;
- to forewarn about changes that may lie ahead, especially the enormous difference it makes when a couple become parents;
- to think about how they will support each other in the difficult times: times when there are money problems, sickness, loss, exhaustion, hard decisions;
- to discuss relationships with their families and with friends.

Decide on the best arrangements

Since most clergy receive, as part of their ordination training, some guidance on how to conduct marriage preparation, perhaps individual sessions with a minister should be the norm? Or is it better to run courses for groups of couples which are jointly led by ordained and lay people?

It is impossible to give a definitive answer, because everything depends on the particular situation. The possibilities depend to a large extent on the number of marriages that take place in a particular area. In a cluster of small villages there may be only half a dozen weddings spread out over a year, so it is not possible – even if a minister would like to do this – for preparation sessions to involve several couples together. On the other hand, in an urban area there may be the opposite difficulty: there are just too many weddings for a minister to give adequate time to preparing couples individually. So it is either delegated to others – or not done at all.

Individual meetings do not have to be embarrassing, as suggested in one of the quotations at the beginning of this chapter. Nor do they have to be unstructured. One minister who sees couples by himself asks them to come for two meetings:

At the first one I have three aims:

to put the couple at their ease, so that they feel able to discuss freely their expectations and concerns: I try to keep the whole approach relatively light and not without humour;

to talk with them about their hopes for their marriage and to see how far these hopes are shared – or divergent;

to raise with them possible areas of difficulty and how to deal with these.

One method I use is to give them both a sheet with a list of 'hopes', which they begin by looking at separately. I ask them to tick the ones they think most important, cross off any they think don't apply and add any others that are important to them. After doing this on their own they then compare notes and we have a discussion on the results.

In the second session I go through the marriage service with them in detail, emphasising especially the full implications of the promises they will make.

Group courses – pros and cons
There is much to be said for using a team to carry out marriage preparation, including lay people. 'The witness and approach of lay Christians often carries greater impact in today's secular world.'[4]

Ministers may feel they do not have the gifts to carry out the whole of the job themselves. Having one or two others to work with can feel like a reassuring safety net: 'Sometimes I have been fearful that some of my own anxiety – and cynical realism – will spill over into the evening and be threatening for couples who are looking at each other through rose-tinted spectacles. Working with a team or partner means we can monitor each other's moods and if necessary re-dress the balance at the next session.'

Sometimes a couple are well known in their local church and the minister they speak to has a good idea of how well they already understand what marriage means. But more often the couple are 'unchurched' and the minister has to gauge what their starting point may be. Throw several such couples together on a course and although it may be new and exciting for some, for others it may feel socially awkward – or seem like a waste of time. Again, the difference between couples who are already living together and those who are not may produce either fruitful discussion or uneasy silences.

One minister delegates the preparation sessions to just one carefully chosen pair of lay people, who belong to the marriage preparation group, which is a sub-group of the pastoral team. (All the members of this group are married – though not necessarily to each other.) 'Each couple is invited personally to a friendly evening meeting with a 'preparer' couple. This is kept informal, but the preparers do have a rough structure in mind so that all important matters are covered. After this session the couple are free to ask for another meeting, which they frequently do. The 'preparers' will make a point of greeting the couple in church when their banns are read, will attend the wedding if possible and in any case will send the couple a greetings card from themselves and the whole congregation.'

There are many gains for a couple who attend a course with others. Being open in a group may well help them to talk more freely to each other. In sharing their experiences they will be able to help others as well as learning themselves. Belonging to the group will strengthen them as they embark on this new undertaking and through the group they may well make lasting friendships, supportive in the future. They will be shown that not only ministers, but the whole church, cares about them and wants to offer support and encouragement at this critical time of their lives. They will be helped to make bonds, not just with a particular minister, but with the Christian community. This approach requires restraint by ministers and more 'ministerial work' by the congregation.

It may be difficult, however, to persuade couples to attend a course – even if it is warmly recommended by ministers and by those who have already experienced it. Much will depend on whether they are used to the idea because they have friends who have done something similar. The more pressure is exerted, the more resistant they may feel. Even those who do agree to attend may still have questions and doubts. It will be important to provide an opportunity – either in an individual session with a leader or during the first session of the course – for them to express these. It helps if they receive a sensitively written letter of invitation, together with a leaflet describing the course.

Course content and methods

Courses may have various different emphases. There is likely to be a solid practical component, with a doctor, accountant or lawyer talking and answering questions. Talks may be given on various aspects of marriage, perhaps with several married people speaking about their own experiences. Or more interactive methods may be used – or a mixture of these styles. People with counselling and group skills may act as facilitators, to help the couples to share their feelings and expectations – both between couples and with each other.

The Christian view may be put across more – or less – forcefully. Since it is a *church* wedding that is being planned, most couples will expect and welcome some Christian input. They will accept it as normal practice if each session opens and closes with a time of prayer. This will show them how simple and helpful it is to submit all our activities to God's guiding. It will also provide a natural opening into discussion of the place prayer can have in everyday married life.

One experienced minister feels that couples should be offered questions, rather than statements or advice: 'When we ask questions we must resist the impulse to leap to supply answers, but must follow them with relaxed friendly waiting – even if it takes time for a couple to arrive at real answers.'

In deciding which type of course might be appropriate in a particular local context, some of the available published courses should first be looked at – and the question should be considered: 'How much adaptation, to make it suitable for our church, would the material need?'

* Information and advice about published courses can be obtained from the FLAME (Family Life and Marriage Education) group in each area.

If a course is to be designed to fit local circumstances, a small team should work on this. It would be wise to show the proposed outline to some other colleagues (and also if possible to some couples who have recently been members of such a course) for their comments.

A course in an ecumenical parish

This course, although it has its own emphases and methods, is fairly typical. The broad plan for this course was agreed by an ecumenical group of ministers, who brought in a number of experienced lay people to help.

* Three 'teams' of three people each were formed to lead the courses. In some teams one of the ministers was a member, in others the three were all lay people.
* The courses accepted up to seven couples at a time.

- A course consisted of three sessions, either on three weekday evenings or on one whole Saturday. Each session included a social time over refreshments and a meditative time linked to an appropriate part of the marriage service.
- Those ministers who were not members of the marriage preparation team attended the first session, in order to introduce 'their' couples to the leaders.

Content
Each team decided the aspects of each broad topic on which they wanted to concentrate.

A. BREAKING AND MAKING
What it means to be a person ... letting go of self ... building each other up ... learning between couples ... 'oughts' and how to get rid of them.
Relationships ... their demands ... children ... family, past and present ... dealing with in-laws ... breaking bonds with parents.
Male/female similarities and differences.
Commitment and love.

B. TALKING AND LISTENING
Communication: talking and listening ... how to defuse situations.
Money (as a specific example of an area where communication is important) ... organizing finances.
Sexual life ... how to deal with it ... living with hang-ups.
More on male/female similarities and differences.

C. HOPES AND FEARS
Joys ... fears ... expectations ... difficulties ... goals and fantasies (we must own them) ... coping with change (especially within) ... identifying our philosophy of life ... mechanisms for coping.
What marriage is ... God ... God's intention for marriage ... the Gospel ... looking at the marriage vows ... looking at life beyond the material ... why do you want a church marriage?

Methods

Each team decided the methods they would use, bearing in mind the following guidelines:

- Each leader would use best a method with which they were personally comfortable.
- Participants vary as to which method they learn from best, so it was desirable for teams to offer a variety of methods: this also made the sessions feel lively and stimulating.
- Some methods used were: group work, visual aids, 'chalk and talk', case histories, 'brainstorming' and practical exercises (see Chapter 12).
- An element of 'play', such as a light-hearted icebreaker, was included in each session, to help people to relax.
- Every session was evaluated at its end by both course members and leaders.

Support and training

Leaders' meetings were held regularly at which evaluations, ideas, course materials and hand-outs were shared. Training sessions were arranged when needed, for example for help with skills for leading groups of very disparate people and 'from cold' – groups whose members were not known to the leaders or to each other. There was always much goodwill among all the ministers and course leaders, but even so they found it difficult to be completely open with each other. There were differences among them about marriage theology, which needed to be brought into the open – so eventually they used an outside consultant who helped them to do this creatively.

Preparing the preparers

'We want to find leaders who can offer some guidance for the couples' future life and attitudes in an informal and exploratory atmosphere.'

'Leaders must want to assist individuals to do their own thinking rather than talking to them.'

In this section we shall consider how, when a course is being set
up which is to be led by teams of two or three people, these
leaders can be recruited, trained and supported.

Finding leaders

In one church a working party of lay people was asked to set up
some courses for marriage preparation: 'We began by asking the
clergy to give us names of lay people they felt could be trained
as leaders. We suggested the following guidelines:

- aged 30–50-ish; sincere; flexible
- can see things from the point of view of others
- are not easily embarrassed, shocked or 'thrown' by
  difficulties
- have a sense of humour
- can listen
- can draw others out
- are willing to speak from personal experience where
  appropriate, but with humility, especially about the
  importance of religion in their own lives
- can work with other co-leaders
- feels comfortable with people of various ages and
  backgrounds
- can discuss, when they arise: finance; housing; doing chores;
  sexual behaviour; bringing up children; relations with
  in-laws; factors that help in keeping couples together;
  ways of overcoming problems.'

It is not known whether any such paragons were found, but
perhaps leaders were recruited who possessed at least a few of
these excellent qualities.

Is it helpful to use married couples to lead marriage preparation? On the one hand a couple can demonstrate how their

married relationship works and speak together from first-hand experience of how they have coped with the ups and downs of married life. On the other hand a couple may convey the suggestion that their personal ways of relating and coping are the only right ways. It may be best to recruit leaders who are married, but not to place married couples together in a leadership role.

It can sometimes be acceptable for single people to help with marriage preparation, provided they have the necessary group skills, sensitivity and insight and, most important, are free from hang-ups about their own 'singleness'.

Training leaders

A church member who is experienced in setting up and leading marriage preparation courses explains his church's policy: 'We do not offer any training, as such, for leaders. We just look out for interested, committed Christian married couples and ask them to join us. Usually they don't take a very active role on their first weekend course, just observe and "socialise" and come to the planning and de-briefing meetings we have before and after each course. This seems to work quite well. Those who are interested tend to do their own reading on the subject, and may go to training seminars that are advertised in the press from time to time, but we do not insist on this.' (This account does of course describe a kind of 'training', even if the writer prefers not to call it 'training as such'.)

Some 'preparation' of leaders is essential, even if those invited to take part are already experienced in group work or counselling. Leaders need to be clear about what marriage means, about social changes that have affected attitudes and about the pressures people have to cope with today – as well as possessing a degree of self-understanding and insight into their own relationships.

Leaders should already have experience in leading groups, because this is a skill that cannot be acquired in an instant. It may need some deftness to handle those who are resistant to joining in group exercises or in open discussion: encouraging them to participate, while respecting their freedom. Leaders may also have to deal with participants who dominate the group with their particular worries or who turn out to have serious problems that need to be taken somewhere else. The group exists for discussion, not counselling. Sitting in on some courses that are already running, if necessary in another place (including taking part themselves in any 'exercises' that the couples are asked to do), is useful.

Leaders who are confident in leading a group can be flexible with regard to content. In the limited time available for a course it is not possible to cover everything that might be useful, so the leader has to decide which are the most important areas or adopt a flexible approach – listening to course members and being led by their needs.

One leader explains: 'We have a framework of topics, but we do not stick rigidly to this. We try to be sensitive to what the couples want to discuss. Couples often bring to the group problems that they will also bring to their marriage, for example parental divorce, death of a parent, loss of a job. One can never be certain what subject areas will prevail. But whatever comes up we say "talk about it!" We know too that couples do talk about things between the group sessions.'

A TRAINING SESSION FOR LEADERS

Here is a suggested plan. Similar methods are used for training leaders to those that are experienced by couples on a course.

- Brainstorm on topics likely to come up in discussion with couples.
- Reflect on the preparation (if any) they themselves received.
- Identify the topics that will be most suitable for a group at its beginning and those that should be left until the group has developed some trust.
- Use an exercise giving practice in leading a group – in which it will become apparent that it is best not to rush in with an

account of one's own experience, but to draw participants
out by means of open questions.

* Use a role play, in which two of the trainees act as leaders
  and the rest pair up as 'engaged couples' – to help in
  understanding how people doing a course might feel.
* Include exercises in active listening and in handling conflict
  – similar to exercises that can be used with couples.
* Include a reminder that the leaders will need to reassure
  couples that they are not there to find out more about them
  and report on them – to the clergy or anyone else! They
  will need to emphasize to couples that anything said in the
  course sessions by anyone will be treated as confidential.

Talking about sex

The churches have the reputation, perhaps deserved in the past,
for taking a disapproving attitude towards sex. In marriage
preparation we need to be clear that sex is a good gift from
God – and that we can use it well or badly. It is important to
include discussion of the sexual side of marriage, to handle this
calmly and sympathetically and to encourage openness. Any
embarrassment on the part of the leader about discussing sex
quickly infects couples.

It is specially necessary for leaders to be aware of their own
assumptions and prejudices about sex and sexual activity. If they
have strong moral views they should not reveal them too soon,
though in the end leaders must be free to say what they think,
while making it clear that they respect other views. If the team
of leaders have differing views among themselves, and allow this
to be seen, it may be quite liberating to the participants, giving
them 'permission' to come out with their own doubts, questions and perhaps unconventional viewpoints.

Support for leaders

Usually support is found in the meetings that are held to plan
and debrief the course sessions. All ministers should be invited
to at least some of these meetings. Leaders should also be

encouraged to find personal support from someone who will act as their supervisor, to talk over their work and to help with appraisal.

The 'church council' should from time to time receive a report about the marriage preparation process. The church magazine can also include some account of it, so that the congregation as a whole knows what is going on and who is involved. This will encourage them to take an interest and to give their support by praying for the leaders and the couples.

Leaders should always continue to learn – from their own experience, from the couples, from fellow team members, from further training meetings – and from their own reading. Many excellent books are available on all aspects of marriage, listening, counselling and group work. Leaders can also be encouraged to attend any seminars offered by their diocese or district, or by such organizations as Scripture Union or the Church Pastoral Aid Society. Training is never completed.

When does marriage preparation start?

All through this chapter it has been assumed that 'preparation for marriage' refers to specific, short-term preparation in advance of a wedding. But in reality people are 'prepared' for marriage from an early age: in their homes, at school, in youth groups, by watching television – and particularly by what they see around them as living examples of marriage – bad and good.

This places a great responsibility on parents, teachers, ministers and church members – and perhaps especially on those of us who are blessed with happy marriages – to commend marriage to the young people of a generation that has largely become disillusioned with public and social institutions. Younger people often say that they cannot see any point in having 'a piece of paper' that evidently does not guarantee lasting commitment.

What we can tell them is that the Christian churches do offer help to those thinking about marrying, *help that is generally not coming from anywhere else*, help with practical plans, help with relationships, the help that comes from friends who care, and the help that comes from seeing ourselves in the light of the care and love of God, reflected by Jesus Christ.

Let me not to the marriage of true minds
  Admit impediments. Love is not love
Which alters when it alteration finds,
  Or bends with the remover to remove.
O, no, it is an ever-fixèd mark
  That looks on tempests and is never shaken;
It is the star to every wand'ring barque,
  Whose worth's unknown although his height be taken.
Love's not time's fool, though rosy lips and cheeks
  Within his bending sickle's compass come;
Love alters not with his brief hours and weeks,
  But bears it out even to the edge of doom.
    If this be error and upon me proved,
    I never writ, nor no man ever loved.

                  (William Shakespeare)[5]

Story for discussion

8. Graham, Angie and Dawn

TOPICS
- Strains on a marriage
- Getting involved
- Conflicting demands

Graham's story: 'Just after my wife, Angie, and I had got married, we were both starting on professional careers. A friend of Angie's, Dawn, was also starting a job at the same time, but she was single, lived alone and had no family or acquaintances in the area. She became very depressed and Angie felt guilty that Dawn had so little.

Then Angie asked Dawn to stay the weekend – we did not think to set any definite time limit on her visit. But she kept finding excuses to stay on. Initially it was all right, but she soon started to cry when we did not give her our full attention. Eventually Angie and I became very frustrated with the continual presence of our unhappy friend. We wanted to escape and wished we had not got involved. Angie and I took to having disagreements when we were not with Dawn. We didn't enjoy having these insights into Dawn's depression. It was contagious and we were vulnerable.

Eventually Dawn did move out. I hope she benefited from staying with us, but I still don't know if we were foolish to get so closely involved with someone. With hindsight I think we took a risk with our marriage, as we had only been married a few weeks, but taking risks is part of caring.

Discussion

1   Should we get involved in caring for someone who is in need, even at the risk of endangering other relationships?
2   If Graham and Angie had talked to you to when they first became worried about Dawn, what suggestions would you have made?
3   How could the church have helped in this situation?

BAPTISM: CHILDREN
AND PARENTS

'There are just too many baptisms every month for it to be possible for me to follow them all up.' (A minister)

'We have a garden with an old damson tree in it, which produces masses of fruit every summer. I usually manage to make some jam, but most of the fruit just falls and is left to go bad and I think "what a waste!" ' (A church member)

'Sophie is a child who is already so blessed in so many ways. But I want something more for her than earth can afford. My prayer for her today is that she will come to have that inner joy and confidence which comes from knowing that God is her father and Jesus her master, friend and guide.' (From a baptism sermon)[1]

The churches are like gardens with overloaded damson trees. In all our towns and villages, estates and suburbs, parents continue to ask for baptism for their babies. They want the best for their children – and they recognize, often without putting it into words, that they can find 'the best' through bringing them to church. These parents present local churches with many opportunities for continuing contact with young families, yet it often happens that these families receive from their churches little or nothing in the way of long-term friendship, support, teaching or nurture – so they drift away. What a waste.

Different approaches to baptism

Churches that practise 'infant baptism' differ widely in their baptism policy. Some aim to restrict baptism to children whose parents meet certain conditions; others accept any child for whom baptism is requested; most invite parents to take part in preparation in some form. Whatever line is taken, it helps in putting the policy across if it has been discussed by the church's council and is understood by church members.

Today the responsibility for children in the church is increasingly seen to lie not just with the parents, but with the whole community: with what is often optimistically referred to as 'the church family'. Therefore many churches have given up holding private baptisms. Baptisms take place instead within the main Sunday service, so that the whole congregation can say to the child, *'We welcome you!'* In this way the congregation is committed to welcoming the child and to encouraging and helping the parents.

In churches which minister to a large population, however, this is not a practical possibility. The church building is often not big enough to hold several extra groups of relatives and friends in addition to the regular congregation. Churches find various different ways of meeting this situation. Sometimes there is a special Sunday afternoon baptism service once a month. The newly-baptized – which may include both children and adults – are then formally welcomed at the main service on the following Sunday.

Everyone can be involved

The clergy often cannot manage, on their own, to visit, look after and 'prepare' two, three or even more 'baptism families' every week. So a team of lay people may be recruited, to do the initial visits to families, lead preparation sessions, offer both encouragement and practical help to parents and keep in touch with them afterwards – as friends who are sometimes known as 'church godparents'.

A few churches (including the parish church in Braxton and its minister, Harry, whom we met in Chapter 3) are now using Documented Management Systems (DMS). This is a grand name for what is really a common-sense way of making sure that 'every member ministry' becomes a reality. The procedures in all parts of church life, including baptism, are first discussed and agreed by those who will be carrying them out, and then they are written down. Each person who is involved plays a part in working out how things should be done and knows exactly what they are responsible for – and also knows how their own contribution dovetails into the whole. The 'documents' are made available for all to look at, so that anyone in the church can comment and make suggestions.[2]

Harry explains: 'Using DMS for baptisms means that parents and families get the sense that they are being properly and thoughtfully looked after and receiving a real welcome – receiving "quality ministry". Above all, having the procedures written down makes it easy, from time to time, to review how things are going – and to make changes in the light of experience.'

Lay involvement usually requires a baptism team, made up of people who are good at relating to families. They may learn the job of baptism visiting by first shadowing an already experienced member of the team at the initial visit to parents. If the family are not already church attenders, the main purpose of this visit is to make a friendly contact. The visitor also finds out how much they know about baptism, whether they have been baptized themselves (not essential for parents), whether godparents have been chosen and whether they are suitable (it is essential for godparents to have been baptized). There is an application form to be filled in; and a date and time for the baptism and for a preparation session to be agreed.

Next the parents are shown a copy of the baptism service. There is a discussion about what will happen in the service, what it all means and, in particular, the meaning of the promises which parents and godparents will make. It is explained that after the baptism the church will keep in touch with them in various ways. They are encouraged to ask questions, to which the visitor tries to give simple and practical answers. There may be a video to lend to parents, together with various leaflets to help them to understand more clearly what baptism does – and does not – do. One minister has put together for parents a pack of attractive A4 sheets explaining everything.

Alternatives to baptism

Some churches offer an alternative to baptism, which is known as a 'thanksgiving' or 'dedication' service. Parents may be given a choice of three possible ways forward.

1 If they do not feel they can make the promises at the moment, they can choose not to go ahead – and this is seen as an honest and positive decision.
2 They can opt for a service of 'dedication'.
3 They can decide on baptism.

Churches that do not believe in the practice of infant baptism usually offer a dedication service for babies and children.

After the baptism

After the baptism – or dedication – has taken place, the baptism team are responsible for demonstrating to the families that the church welcomes and cares about them. The visitor, who has become a friend by now, drops in to see how things are going. 'How is Jason getting on? Oh, isn't he coming on well! How is he sleeping? You must be feeling tired … I do sympathize. Are you worried about anything? Is there anything I can do to help?' The team arranges for a card to be given to the child on the anniversary of the baptism.[3] Sometimes they arrange for all the children who have been baptized in the past year, with their parents and godparents, to be invited to a reunion service and party.

There is a another way by which members of baptism families can be given spiritual help and led towards fuller commitment. A little time after the baptism, those parents who have not themselves been baptized – and also godparents, if they live locally – are invited to an occasion at which the possibility of baptism (and confirmation in some traditions) is suggested. One minister says that every year this results in at least one or two adults going forward for baptism and confirmation. Again, lay people can play a part – by making this suggestion to their relatives and friends and by helping to lead the preparation.

Another minister takes a similar view: 'When people are challenged about baptism, my experience is that, more often than not, they reply that they have always wanted to be christened, but never known what to do about it. Often their parents had never taken them to church and they were frightened to come forward.'[4]

'Church godparents'

All of us who are church members are, in a real sense, 'godparents' to every baby, child or adult who is baptized or dedicated in our church. We have a responsibility to make friends with them, to nurture them in body, mind and spirit, and to pray faithfully for them. If we do all this, as best we can, less of the fruit will be wasted. The 'church family' will become a reality — and the Kingdom of God will be brought closer.

Two stories for discussion

9. Shirley, Clive, Peter and Helen

TOPICS
- Baptism
- Having doubts
- Conflicting feelings
- The role of a minister

Shirley and Clive are a young couple, with a small baby, Peter. They want to have him baptized, so Helen, one of the ministers, visited them to talk about it. Shirley had a lot of questions in her mind, so she asked if she could join the 'Christian basics' course that was just starting in the parish.

She has now attended two sessions of the course, but has found it difficult. Helen noticed that Shirley was looking worried, so the next day she called to see her and encouraged her to talk about the course.

'Well, I feel out of it,' Shirley confessed, 'I keep hearing things like "Jesus died to save us from our sins and rose again to show us that he has conquered death" and I wonder what this means to starving families in Africa. I feel I stick out like a sore thumb in the group.

'Oh dear, I'm in a muddle about my life generally ... it's been a wonderful experience having a baby, but I do miss my job ... and yet I feel so tired I don't know if I could cope with it now. It's too difficult to get to church in time on Sunday mornings, especially as Clive isn't interested in coming. But anyway I'm fed up with listening to stuff I don't really believe in any more. Oh dear, how shocked my parents would be if they could hear me!'

Discussion

- Should Peter be baptized?
- What are Shirley's needs at the moment?
- Can Helen do anything more to help Shirley?

10. Peggy, Jim and Jennifer

TOPICS
- Support by the church family
- Values
- Parents and teenagers

Peggy is married to Jim and they have a daughter, Jennifer, who is aged twelve. Recently Peggy has had some worries about Jennifer. In the last week there have been some heated arguments about her wish to possess very expensive boots of a particular brand name. She claims that everyone else in her class at school has them.

Jim has told Jennifer that her values are all wrong — as a Christian girl she shouldn't be giving this so much importance. She ought to see that what matters is character, not clothes. He is disappointed that she can't stand up to the other girls. Those sort of boots look dreadful anyway!

Peggy suspects Jim is on the way to alienating Jennifer, but on the other hand she doesn't feel it would be right just to give her the boots — especially as it would make a big hole in the month's housekeeping money. Peggy is hoping that she and Jim will soon get some time alone together, when they can discuss the problem.

Discussion

1   What should Peggy say to Jim?
2   How should they handle the situation with Jennifer?
3   What support might they find from the church family?

WORSHIP AND BELONGING

'When you meet for worship, each of you contributes a hymn,
some instruction, a revelation, an ecstatic utterance, or the inter-
pretation of such an utterance. All of these must aim at one thing:
to build up the church. Let all be done decently and in order.'
(1 Corinthians 14:26, 40 New English Bible)

'Worship is loving God in the presence of one another, and loving
one another in the presence of God.' (Betty Pulkingham)[1]

'What the most reticent worshipper in the back pew thinks and
does is of as much interest to God as the thoughts and actions of
those who have well defined leadership roles.' (The Church of
Scotland's Panel on Worship)[2]

'We had family weekends, at which thousands of people came
together, and were singing and dancing until one in the morning.
We need imaginative liturgists to create forms of worship meaningful to the people — free, Spirit-filled services, with the rhythms
black Africans love.' (Most Rev. Winston Ndungane)[3]

*'I remember my mother coming to church with me once and sitting
with tears running down her face. "I could never go there again,"
she said later, "it upsets me too much."' (Monica Furlong)*[4]

Does going to church make you feel better —
or worse?

Our values

'Worship' is not a word that is normally heard in casual chat in
the bus queue. Yet it describes a dimension of everyone's life.
'Worship' refers to our values: to what we think is important
and how we express our feelings about that. Saturday afternoon
at a football match; Sunday lunch with the family; these could
be called 'worship' in this wide sense, because in these ways
people are supporting something that is important for them.
When people attend a church service they similarly demonstrate
that they regard this as a worthwhile activity, that it is important to them to be there, to spend time in becoming aware of
God's presence, in thinking about what life means, in expressing
gratitude — and to do these things together with others.

Worship together happens mainly on Sunday but in many
churches it happens on weekdays also. There are, as well, the
baptisms, weddings and funerals and all the special events which
may include: the school harvest festival; Remembrance Sunday
and other national days; the Carol Service and Nativity Play; the
Women's World Day of Prayer; the Christingle Service with
candles and oranges; Mothering Sunday with the giving of posies;
Taize services; healing services; 'guest' or 'seeker' services. This
chapter focuses on the main Sunday worship in a local church —
which might, for example, be a service of Holy Communion or
of Breaking Bread, a Family Service or Morning Praise — but
most of what is said applies equally to other occasions.

Sunday morning worship varies widely in different churches —
even where similar forms of service are used: from 'high'
through 'middle-of-the-road' to 'low'; from lively and musical

to quiet and meditative; from a city street to a country hamlet; from formal to informal. But within this range many similar opportunities occur to help each other towards a more vivid awareness and understanding of God's care – and practical guidelines can be found that work well in any setting.

Going to church

'Day and night without ceasing they sing: "Holy, holy, holy, the Lord God the Almighty..." They cast their crowns before the throne, singing: "You are worthy, our Lord and God, to receive glory and honour and power, for you created all things..." ' (Revelation 4: parts of 8, 10, 11).

Ministers and leaders regard worship as, above all, an offering to God – identifying with the 'elders around the throne' in the great vision of worship in Revelation; appreciating Paul's frequent emphasis on thankfulness: 'with gratitude in your hearts sing psalms, hymns and spiritual songs to God' (Colossians 3:16b), and responding to Evelyn Underhill's description of worship as: 'the response of the creature to the Eternal'.[5]

When lay people come to church, they are often more concerned initially about their own needs than about 'the Eternal': they come – often as a weekly routine – to find friendship or comfort or strength to go on, or 'to get things in proportion'. The minister of a church in a large town says he is often moved and impressed when people tell him how much help for living they have received through coming to church: 'I couldn't have got through that bad time if I hadn't managed to get to church.'

It is easy for ministers and pastors who are responsible for organizing and delivering pastoral care sometimes to forget that it is *God* who cares for people. In a church service we are reminded that in all our caring for each other we are participating in God's love, helping people to know for themselves the redeeming work of Christ. Thus the words used in corporate worship need to be linked with everyday reality: the reality of God's love being expressed through the practical actions of people: in visiting, listening, doing chores, being alongside each other in countless ways.

Those who bring their needs to church find there many kinds of 'pastoral care' – which are all reflections of God's care. Individuals can only give their response to that love when they have become aware of God's hand in their lives. Paul wrote of how Christ had first taken hold of him – 'made me his own' (Philippians 3:12) – and how he then wanted nothing else but to 'press on toward the goal for the prize of the heavenly call of God in Christ Jesus'. 'Wanting' soon leads people into longing for a closer friendship with God, a daily conforming to God's plan, thanking, rejoicing; and then a turning outwards and beyond, in love for God and for all fellow creatures – in an upward spiral of learning and growing.

In its worship, as in all its activities, the Church can help everyone to experience this awareness of God. It can happen in many different ways and places, but in church we can expect it to happen frequently and powerfully.

Trying to please everyone

People are looking for many different things when they come to church. Some of these differences may depend on their temperament, on what is going on in their lives, on how regularly they attend and on what they have been used to in the past. Among those present at a service on any Sunday, there are sure to be some people who are trying to commune quietly with God, others who long for colour and excitement.

'I love the beautiful Prayer Book words, which I've known since I was a child.'

'I like to feel stretched. I feel excited when I meet new ideas.'

'It bothers me when they keep changing the way things are done in church. I like to know what to expect.'

'An anthem by Bach or Handel, beautifully sung, that's what carries me away.'

'It helps me if I can *see* the stories about Jesus, so I always watch when a Bible film is shown on TV. Our church has a drama group and sometimes the "readings" are acted out, which makes them come alive.'

'I feel inspired when someone gives a talk about their own experience of getting to know Jesus in their lives.'

'I can't bear it if someone gets up and displays their feelings to the whole congregation – it makes me die of embarrassment.'

'I'm always hoping I'll make some real Christian friends through coming to church.'

'I just want to be left alone ... I come to think and get some peace ... I don't want strangers breezing up to me.'

There may be someone who has come back to the church after a long gap, needing comfort at a time of bereavement and perhaps puzzled by the changes since the last time she came; an engaged couple, excited about hearing their banns read; a group of teenagers; young parents wanting to do their best for their children, but worried when they make a noise; several single people in mid-life; a good many who are retired; at least one person who comes in a wheelchair. There is usually a majority who are regular attenders; often there are also a few who are dipping their toes into the waters of formal worship for the first time.

How can those who have responsibility for the worship in a local church possibly meet all these different – even conflicting – expectations? Even in a big church where a varied menu of services and meetings can be provided – let alone in a church with fewer resources – it cannot be achieved. Ministers may decide that in this situation it is their role to make the decisions. They may well settle for 'continuity' – sticking to whatever pattern is already in place and therefore familiar and expected. Or they may decide to explore radical change.

The planning of worship

What matters is that the contribution of worship to pastoral care is recognized and the planning of it shared. Most ministers, in the nature of things, are rarely on the receiving end of worship and most lay people hesitate to tell a minister what they think about a service, because they are afraid of seeming to be personally critical. Usually the only comments ministers hear are those made by one or two who are confident and vocal and usually concerned to resist change – or, occasionally, determined to force it through. If only to ensure that ministers get to hear a balanced range of views, it is helpful if the responsibility for the planning of worship is shared by a group which meets regularly.

A 'worship group' could give some time to thinking about basic questions such as:

- What is worship in church for? Should it be aiming primarily to give people comfort and reassurance or should it also challenge them to change their lives?
- Who is it for? Is it primarily for those who already belong or is it meant to speak also to 'fringers' and 'beginners'?
- How can the different needs of the young and the old be met?
- Can 'worship' in church enable the leaders to care for the people who come?
- Can it help the people who come to care for each other?
- Can it be a power-house for pastoral care in the surrounding community?
- How can Sunday worship give people support for their weekday lives?

A 'worship group' will also make practical plans, grounded on a continual review of everything that happens in church: considering the details of how, from the moment people set foot in the building – or even in the churchyard – to the moment when they leave to go home, they are cared for, nourished and inspired. This may be expressing an ideal, but at least there will be a strategy for pastoral care through the church's worship.

Music

Bishop Michael Marshall has called music 'the bicycle of the liturgy'.[6] Music is certainly central to pastoral care through worship. Through the church's music everyone can be encouraged to join in 'raising the roof' with God's praise. But just because music is so important it can be a source of difficulty. Church members often have strong views about musical style and about the kinds of music they find uplifting – or irritating. They feel emotional about the choice of hymns and songs. They may be upset if they consider that the 'wrong tune' is being played.

In many churches today, particularly in country areas, it may be a struggle to provide any music at all, never mind music of good quality. Organists have become scarce. Choirs have become smaller or have disappeared entirely. There is reluctance to use recorded music. On the other hand, in places where the music is strong there are sometimes disagreements between ministers and the organist or choir leader. Any musician is sure to care deeply about the quality of musical performance and may find it hard to accept that this must sometimes come second to other considerations – such as participation by the whole congregation, or choosing music that suits the aims of a family service or youth service.

Pastors need to make opportunities to talk sympathetically with the music director – and to listen pastorally, whether the problems are about never having enough time with the family because of always being in church, or about feeling disappointed by the poor attendance record of some choir members, or feeling sad that plans to perform an anthem by Haydn have fallen through, or being put out by the suggestion that an extract from 'Godspel' would be more relevant.

It always helps if the music director is encouraged to play a full part in the planning of the worship. Where there are continuing difficulties, compromises can usually be found in the end, provided that time is made for calm discussion. Perhaps an agreement can be reached for the musical menu to have some variety of style.

Welcoming

How does your church appear to people as they arrive, especially to newcomers? What message do the churchyard and the notice-board convey? Is this a well-kept, well-loved church? Is its programme clearly set out so that everyone can see what is available and feel encouraged to come along? Is the entrance dark and forbidding or bright and welcoming? Do people have to push open a heavy door in order to get in?

What impression do people get when they first step inside to attend a service? When people are new they do not know where they are supposed to sit (and this can be specially difficult if they arrive late). A steward may give them a pile of books and wave vaguely in the direction of the pews. Probably they sit down near the back and hope no one will notice that they don't know which book to use or how to find the right place. The service begins and there are many hurdles. It is difficult to be sure when to stand, sit or kneel. The service book is complicated and they are not sure what is going on. Someone goes up to the front and reads from the Bible, but the passages do not seem to connect with anything else. There is a sermon, but it is full of mysterious words like 'outreach' and 'redemption'. If there is Communion, they wonder when to get up and go forward to the rail, or even whether they are entitled to do so.

When at last the end comes, they may hang about a little, hoping to have a chat with someone. But the minister is caught up in a deep conversation and most people are bustling out, anxious to get home. A few seem to have obtained cups of coffee from somewhere and are standing around chatting, obviously knowing each other or immersed in church business. It seems impossible to break into any of these 'huddles', so the newcomers or occasional attenders give up and slip away.

This may seem an exaggerated account, but it reflects what often happens. It is so easy for newcomers to feel that they stick out as outsiders. One newcomer describes her feelings: 'As I have no church background at all, I had no idea what to do. I felt as if I had crashed someone else's party.' It is so easy for those in the 'inner ring' of a church, being preoccupied with church affairs, to appear to brush others off. A university teacher describes how he attended a 'well-known evangelical church in London', because he wanted to gain a greater understanding of the religious attitudes of those of his students who were Christians. After the service, hoping to ask some questions, he approached the lay pastor who had led the service, only to be told he would 'do best to read our newspaper'. He continues, 'in that newspaper the minister had written "Nobody can be ridden rough-shod over. Nobody fails to count." After that service I certainly felt I had failed to count.'[7] Enthusiastic singing, sincere prayers and inspired preaching are not enough without a warm personal response.

In many churches, however, great trouble *is* taken to make sure that everyone receives that 'kindly personal response' and can feel at home. In some churches, especially where the congregation is large, there is a 'welcome desk', with a display of helpful leaflets, books and tapes, and someone behind it to give an encouraging smile and offer assistance. Sometimes the stewards are known as 'welcomers' and make a point of shaking hands with everyone, regulars and newcomers alike, as they arrive.

During worship the whole congregation – not only the pastor and stewards – can help by developing an attitude of openness to God and to others. If those who come regularly are conscious of God's loving presence throughout the service, this can 'infect' others around them with an awareness of God's loving care for them also. When people have taken their seats for a service (ideally in good time, so that there is a chance to settle down without rush and to pray quietly first), they can smile in a friendly way at the person sitting next to them and perhaps ask, 'How are you?' or, 'What sort of week have you had?'

If a person seems to need help it is best to say, 'We can meet after the service if you want to,' or, 'I think Mary Smith could help you – if you like I'll arrange for you to talk to her later.' Vera, who is an occasional church attender, recommends that an 'escape route' should always be provided. She finds that if someone says, 'After the service ends I'll meet you by the bookstall,' she may feel quite alarmed. A more sensitive approach would be: 'If you want to know more about anything or need any help look out for me after the service.'

Our needs

'Church again. My prayer is now only "Here I am again. Show me what to do. Help me to do it."'[8]

We all come to church as needy – even broken – people, with many of our needs in common. It is in the details of how people prefer church services to be conducted that they differ, rather than in the basic human needs they bring to church. Here are some of them.

- To be known personally
- To be oneself
- To belong
- To feel safe
- To learn
- To get a wider view
- To be stimulated and challenged
- To refresh the inner life
- To glimpse God's glory

- To find healing and a chance to start again
- To renew commitment

To be known personally

Everyone wants to be recognized as an individual; to be known and remembered. People want a place where they can be themselves, where they do not have to pretend they are 'fine, thanks!', when really they are full of worries. One of the advantages of a small church is that it is easier for all who come to know that they count. In a large congregation they are more likely to feel that no one notices them. This does not mean, however, that people want a spotlight turned on them. They certainly do not want to be singled out in an embarrassing way. As one minister says: 'There is always a danger of people feeling targeted or manipulated. I am wary of picking on newcomers, who would rather not be called out in front and introduced to hundreds of people. As leaders we try to be as gentle as we can with people. We just desperately try to be open to God – and take risks when they are needed.'[9] Another minister, with a large congregation, says: 'At the beginning of every service we have a few minutes of "introducing yourselves" – and we have lots of coffee at every event.'

People want to be accepted and valued as they are. Especially in deprived areas, people today often have no sense at all of their own value, can see little point in life, have no hope of breaking out of the cycle of dependence in which they are caught. A minister living and working on a large housing estate on the outskirts of a big city says, 'The challenge for the church is to make people feel valued ... and therefore confident to live out their faith in adverse circumstances.' It is in church – though not only in church – that the Christian message, with its relevance for those without hope, is proclaimed: that each person has value for no other reason than that Christ died for them; that God accepts and loves us for what we *are* – not for what we *do* or achieve, nor for how we *look* or *behave*.

If, in its community life, a church is reflecting God's love, then everyone who comes must be accepted without conditions. They should not feel that people keep their distance because they are not dressed like everyone else, do not behave or talk as others do. But can acceptance really be without conditions? What if a person comes into the church who is unkempt, noisy, violent, under the influence of drink or drugs? This question could usefully be discussed by all those who do 'belong', or at least be given an airing in the church council.

The conventional answer must be that 'accepting a person' does not mean allowing them to behave exactly as they please, making everyone around them suffer as a result. That would not in the long run, it could be argued, be the most loving response. But in practice, when a crowd of youngsters arrive for Midnight Mass on Christmas Eve, ten minutes late and the worse for drink, and are told they cannot come in, they do *not* feel loved, cared for and accepted. The message they are likely to remember is that they were *not* acceptable to 'the Church'. What can be done? Perhaps someone could carry out some follow-up later, to find out who they are and get to know them.

To be oneself

'African philosophy has no Western-style dualism; it makes no distinction between the sacred and the profane. Everything comes from God; all life is one. We must make good use of that.'[10]

People often feel that it is not only appropriate to be better dressed in church than in their 'normal' lives, but also that they have to put on a special 'front'. This may make it more difficult for them to be, in the church ambience, open and honest and true to their 'real' selves. In church services there is often a failure to give recognition to the whole of people's lives, rather than just the small part of it they feel they can bring to church on Sunday.

The young couple with the double-buggy, containing baby and toddler, have a weekday life running a stressful business, with all the problems of fitting it in with the care of their children. The single young man who turns up occasionally is a policeman working unsocial hours in an undermanned station, where he worries because – like the minister – he knows the area cannot be covered properly. Then there is John, who has lost his job and is feeling angry and frustrated and ashamed: 'I put on a suit for church and try to look normal, but inside I feel a freak.' He finds that church members often make hasty assumptions about everyone having a conventional job – or any job. 'I don't know what to say when someone who is trying to be friendly asks me what I do.' He suggests that more tactful openings, making fewer assumptions, might be: 'What sort of week have you had?' or, 'What sort of life do you have?'

The following conversation took place after a Sunday service. Ruth is a member of the 'worship committee'. Claire comes to church occasionally.

Claire: 'No one in the church bothers about working mothers. The services don't seem to relate to the sort of problems we have in our lives.'

Ruth: 'Would it help if the working world was mentioned more often in the prayers?'

Claire: 'No, I don't think I would like that. When I do manage to get to church I want to escape from the rest of my life ... the last thing I want is to be reminded of work problems!'

Claire, like many others, has a confused mixture of desires: she wants to find in church a different perspective, by getting away from the problems of her weekday life. At the same time she wants to feel that the church cares about her 'weekday' as well as her 'Sunday' self.

Churches need to look for ways of enabling people to bring all of themselves into their worship. There is no need for spiritual 'nude bathing', but people can be assured that they do not have to hide anything from God. A few words of introduction to the 'confession' and a short time of silence at that point can help. The intercessions can provide opportunities for voicing people's real concerns: weekday activities of all kinds can be mentioned – and honoured as 'ministries' that are as valuable as those exercised within the programme of the church. Some particularly urgent needs can be stressed by recognizing national days such as 'Unemployment' or 'Homelessness' Sundays.

In a real sense the church goes on existing throughout the week, but dispersed in the separate lives of all its members. On Sunday all that experience in daily life can be gathered up and offered to God. Strength can be renewed, as we pray: 'Send us out in the power of your Spirit to live and work ...'[11]

To belong

Most people are members of various different groups: their family, their street or village, their workplace, the bowls club or the hockey team, the horticultural society, an evening class in pottery or computing, the school governors, the district council, the local branch of a political party. But there is a difference between formal membership and real 'belonging'. If you 'belong' it means that you spend time with people with whom you have something in common, are cared for by them and contribute to their care, feel some degree of loyalty to the group, have the chance, if you wish, to play a part in running it and have a voice in its affairs.

Joining a local church means becoming also part of a far wider scene – nothing less than 'the whole company of earth and heaven', the Church Universal, down the centuries and across the world – even though most of the time people are hardly conscious of all this. Indeed when we look round us on Sunday morning it may be difficult to imagine it. The joy – and sometimes also the problem – of belonging to the church locally is that we do not choose the other people who attend. A congregation is a mixture of people who may have little else in common beyond their loyalty to Jesus Christ.

Being a member, even in a formal sense, is important for many who remain on the fringe and never enter fully into the life of the church community. The historian G.M. Trevelyan is said to have declared, 'I'm an agnostic, but a C.of E. agnostic of course!'[12] He was not untypical. Many others, however, do want to come in from the fringe and enter the circle: to 'belong' fully.

In practical terms, most people who do join the church want to contribute actively. They want to be sure that any gift they offer, whether of their money, time or talents, is appreciated and used. 'They announced they wanted more lesson readers and I did offer, but no one has ever taken it up.' If church officers appeal for help and receive an offer (or if an offer of help comes unasked for), it should be responded to within a reasonable time, so that the person feels appreciated. Wide participation will also prevent the development of 'cliques' or an 'inner ring'.

On some occasions the planning of a particular service – or of any other church activity – can be given to a different group from usual: for example, to a home group, the youth fellowship or the junior church, or the group who came together for the last church 'Away-day'. They can work out a theme, choose readings, hymns and prayers and some of their members can lead various sections of the service. For those who lack confidence, even reading out a notice can begin to make them more sure of themselves.

Drama and visual aids can help more people to become actively involved – especially today when so much learning is done visually. 'The time has now come to rebuild, recover and reclaim a meaningful symbolism, dramatically presented, which speaks to the imagination of our age; which people can follow, but even more important, in which people can participate.'[13]

The church is one of the few places where young people can be helped to believe that they are important, have gifts, are needed. It is especially sad that in many churches the few youngsters who come with their parents to begin with are often alienated in the end because they are made to feel the opposite: that they are of no importance. Many youngsters enjoy taking part in a play, sketch or mime – so drama is a particularly good way of giving young people a chance to contribute.

When a service is advertised as a 'Family Service' it should be made clear that this refers to the 'family of the church' and is not intended to exclude those who come on their own, are single or have no children. Services for 'Mothering Sunday' are often misunderstood and assumed to be intended only for those who are parents. Churches need to think carefully about how they can prevent these feelings of exclusion that are so easily aroused. Careful wording of publicity material or a change of name can help. Some churches avoid the name 'Family Service', using instead terms such as 'Parish Communion' or 'Morning Worship Together'.

If there is a social time over coffee or tea after the service is over, people can catch up with each other's lives during the past week and ask for or offer help. The rotas for church cleaning and lesson reading can be sorted out and dates for meetings fixed. All this is useful, but 'regulars' need to be specially alert during this time to notice anyone who might be feeling shy or left out and introduce them to others.

There are always some people who claim to be 'loners', or 'non-joiners'. When 'the Peace' is exchanged, for example, there are usually a few who, for all sorts of personal reasons, do not wish to make contact with others – and this should be respected. But in many churches most people wander about for a few minutes, seeking out both friends and strangers, giving each other warm and genuine smiles and handshakes, with a hug and a kiss if they feel like it. Where there is already a sense of community, people often find they can forget their normal reserve and let themselves go. 'The Peace' can become a powerful visual sign that, at a deep level as they approach God's table, everyone belongs together.

To feel safe

People need to feel secure: they do not want to spend the whole time wondering what is going to happen next. 'Stage directions' printed on a leaflet or service sheet are helpful. People want to feel confident that the person leading the service is clear as to what it is about and where it is going. The minister's own manner can create – or destroy – confidence. A few sentences of welcome and a sincerely warm smile at the beginning can work wonders in creating trust.

People feel safe with what is familiar and expected. The regular rhythm of 'the church's year' can provide a reassuringly familiar framework for life. This does not mean that everything must stay the same for ever, but it does mean that there should be good reasons for changes and that trouble should be taken to explain them.

In one large church the minister suggested changing the time of the main service on Sunday morning from 10.00 a.m. to 9.30 a.m. One reason for this was that it would enable some families to come whose children had to go to games practice in the second half of Sunday morning. The church council agreed and the new timing was introduced. A great fuss ensued: elderly people felt they were being trampled on, since they needed an unrushed start to Sunday; working people felt they deserved their 'lie in'; those on the sidesmen's rota, who had not been consulted, felt resentful.

In another church the choir wanted to start holding a 'Taizé service', to replace evensong once a quarter, and this was announced. The regular congregation for evensong, small but faithful, did not know anything about 'Taizé' and felt they were being pushed aside.

The vicar of a group of village churches decided that the elements at Communion should in future be distributed by lay people – which had not happened in those churches before. He had two reasons for this: it would speed things up and save elderly people, in particular, from having to wait a long time before receiving; and it would provide a visual symbol of the church as one body. But these reasons remained inside his own mind. He did not communicate them to those who came, so the change caused some distress. A few months later he wanted to try using a modern version of the service once a month. This time he took care to explain to everyone the reasons why he wanted them to try out the new version. The result was that they were willing to give it a fair trial.

It may seem easier, when something new is planned, just to start without the hassle of explaining. But every minute of time invested in giving reasons, discussing, listening and getting agreement is sure to pay a dividend in future co-operation and goodwill. The reasons for what happens in a church service need to be understood not only by the 'inner ring' – the members of committees and councils – but by everyone in the congregation. This can be achieved by various means: through home groups, the church magazine, special congregational meetings, conversations – at the church door or in the street. When a change is to occur it is often useful to agree on a period of experiment, with reviews from time to time. In due course it is helpful if the reasons for acceptance or rejection are made known, so that the experiment does not just sink without trace.

To get a wider view

When they are in church people want to see their lives from a different slant: to discover a wider and longer view than they can take while they are immersed in the round of everyday life. This will often allay anxiety, but it can also have the opposite effect – of disturbing people's complacency. In church, people may be stimulated to face changes in their lives that they need to make. This may feel upsetting at the time, but later may be seen as part of the unfolding purpose of God.

People discover that in a church service they are in 'fellowship' with a wide group of people, who have come together, not because they share any particular hobby or interest, but because they have in common their Christian faith and a longing to follow Jesus. In church, anyone is likely to find themselves sitting next to someone who is very different from themselves in all kinds of ways. There is no 'table plan' to fix the order in which people receive the bread and wine at Communion; there is no 'officers mess': everyone is mixed up together at the feast.

But there is a dilemma here for every church: how to build up real fellowship, without either putting pressure on people to join in or creating an excluding 'club'. There is no neat solution, but it helps if the core of regular members are at least aware of the danger of exclusiveness, of making others feel left out or unimportant – rather than refreshed by contact with a wide group of 'sisters and brothers'.

There is much in the liturgy that can give us a wider perspective, as the following sentences from a Church of England Communion service show:

> 'With angels and archangels and with all the company of
> heaven ...'
> '...that we and all your Church may receive forgiveness.'
> 'Your will be done on earth as in heaven.'
> 'The body of Christ keep you in eternal life.'
> 'Give us this day our daily bread.'[14]

Bible readings and the sermon can also help. Some words of introduction to the Scripture readings, followed by a few minutes for quiet reflection, can make all the difference to their impact. Sermons can offer helpful and practical exploration of Christian beliefs. Much can be done, even in brief sermons, to give people real enlightenment week by week. Preachers cannot touch the hearts of all their listeners every time, but their words are often used by the Holy Spirit to light up the path for individuals (or confront them) in unexpected ways – which the preacher may never know about.

To learn
'Christian doctrine aims to tell the truth, in order that we may enter into and act upon that truth'.[15]

People often long to know more. They want to understand better what they are saying when they recite the Creed; to learn to pray; to get to know the Bible; to find a Christian approach to the moral problems that increasingly face us all. We may question how much anyone can learn from listening passively to a ten-minute – or even a forty-minute – sermon once a week. We may think that people can learn more if they read at home, join a house group or go along to a study course – perhaps in Lent or Advent. But many people decide they do not have time – or simply do not want – to be involved in any of those things. So we have to make sure that people can learn as much as possible during worship in church on Sunday.

Every part of a service can teach something. Different ways of praying can refresh people's personal prayers. Bible passages, read and explained, can be applied in daily life during the coming week. And as loving community is acted out, God's love is demonstrated.

To experience God's presence and glory

'There was a morning service when something "happened", only who can say what? Worship is like that; sometimes just a rite, now and then an extraordinary thing ... all the happiness of the faith flooded the building and quietened our hearts. Or so I felt, and what is felt is.'[16]

When people come together for worship they are looking for a vision of God's glory, an impression of what is 'beyond' – beyond our physical senses, beyond our mental grasp. It is difficult to describe this precisely. Phrases like 'awareness of the transcendant' or 'a sense of God's presence' do not fully reflect it. Nor is it the same as the 'changed perspective' that has been mentioned earlier, since that is more directly related to our everyday lives, whereas we also yearn for a vision of another life – 'the life of heaven', both for its own sake now and as the goal of our pilgrimage.

A church service can help people towards this experience, through inspiring music, evocative language, and by features of the church building which can kindle feelings of awe and won-der: colourful banners, symbolic stained glass, soaring gothic arches. Appropriate times of silence can be powerful, but need to be used carefully. Some people appreciate long silences, oth-ers cannot cope with them. It can be helpful to punctuate a long silence with short readings or 'thoughts'.

Unfortunately there are also many ways by which a sense of God's presence can be suppressed: by too many mundane direc-tions interrupting the flow or too much chatty informality on the part of the leader. Those in the congregation can kill it by being locked into a self-centred viewpoint. If people fidget and whisper without regard to the needs of those around them; if they want each service to be designed to suit their particular tastes – treating it like a restaurant where they choose from a menu; if they are convinced that they can only worship in a cer-tain style, they are likely to end up feeling frustrated rather than uplifted. People need sensitive help to overcome rigid, uncaring attitudes and to discover that they can find 'Christ in you, the hope of glory' (Colossians 1:27) in unexpected ways – even amidst noisy toddlers and to the sound of simple choruses – and that the Spirit can speak to them through movements of love between *all* God's children.

'*All* God's children'? What about the needs – and the gifts – of people whose sight or hearing is impaired, those who cannot move about easily, who use a wheelchair or have other particu-lar physical or mental difficulties? When a hymn is announced, if the first line is read out it helps people who cannot read the hymn book but who know a lot of hymns by heart. Many simple points like this can make a difference. We should take care to ask them: 'What do you find difficult? What would help?' We should give them the assurance: 'The church family needs you!'

What about those noisy toddlers, shouting and running around, babies crying inconsolably, anxious parents making mat-ters worse by frantically urging them to be quiet? 'I feel that everyone is looking at me, the whole thing is a terrible strain and I get nothing for myself from the service. I wonder every time why I keep coming.'

Then there are the older children, who may feel bored because they do not understand most of the service and at its high point are usually excluded from taking communion. The children's needs — to feel welcomed and safe and valued, to be inspired and stimulated — are not being met either. Many of those who do not have children with them in church find all this distracting and distressing. In such a dismal scenario it is hard for anyone to sense God's presence and nobody feels cared for.

In recent years there has been a welcome movement towards the concept of 'All Age Worship', which helps greatly in balancing the needs of every group. The concept is sound, but experience shows that putting it into practice can have its difficulties. Many useful books are now appearing, however, to help churches to avoid the pitfalls and find the blessings of church services in which *no one* is seen to be 'second class' and therefore assumed to be unsuitable for making a contribution, to receive and to give. At the same time, it is wise to have some services that are not intended for 'all ages', but are meant to meet the needs primarily of adults — perhaps with a session of 'Junior Church' running in parallel. If so, this should be made clear. Practical arrangements, such as providing a properly supervised creche or a 'play corner', also need to be given careful thought, so that pastoral care for children and parents while they are in church can be a reality.

In these and other ways, it can become possible for everyone in the church to know that God is close to them. Everyone can receive, here and now, many glimpses of God's glory.

The chance to start again

People often come to church full of anxiety. Or they may be weighed down by heavy burdens that overshadow their lives: anger, guilt and remorse. They need above all to hear the Good News, the heart of the Christian faith, that we are loved by God unconditionally, without any 'strings'. They need to be assured that God can rescue us, through what Jesus Christ has done, and that God always lets us start again, no matter how tangled up our lives may be. Many others come with a low sense of self-worth. The Good News for them, if they can accept it, is that in the eyes of God they have immense worth.

If confession is given proper weight it can relieve people of these burdens. We confess both the corporate sins, in which we all have some share, and our individual sins, which are the ones that usually weigh us down the most heavily. The whole Bible, but especially the Psalms, is full of expressions of vehement human emotions, including frustration and anger – as well as joy, gratitude and tender affection. People can be encouraged to identify with these expressions and so to unload their own negative feelings.

Many churches arrange for one or two people to be available after the service, in case anyone wants to talk or to pray with someone else. It can also be helpful to have a table at the back with a display of books, booklets and tapes, including recorded sermons – and with someone there who can give guidance. Some churches hold special services for healing, although there is a sense in which every church service is a 'healing service'.

• Prayer for healing will be discussed further in the next chapter.

O worship the Lord in the beauty of holiness

Here the servants of the Servant seek in worship to explore what it means in daily living to believe and to adore.[17]

In worship we come close to the holy God, who provides the motive, the energy and the model for all our practice of caring for each other. Here our faith is strengthened, our inner life renewed. Here we at least try to convey to everyone, including those who have little experience of receiving love, a sense of being welcomed and valued for themselves. Here we try to nourish the spiritual yearnings and insights of young people and to give them a vision of something to live for. If services are conducted sensitively, the 'infection' will spread: the ethos of treating each other with love and respect will permeate the whole of church life – and even begin to colour the life of our communities and workplaces. If services are conducted collaboratively, everyone will see that we are all members together. In our worship in church we give 'quality time' to God. For those who come – with their longing to join in and to find wholeness – we must seek also to make it 'quality time'.

PRAYING TOGETHER

'Then little children were being brought to him in order that he might lay his hands on them and pray.' (Matthew 19:13)

'Then Jesus told them a parable about their need to pray always and not to lose heart...' (Luke 18:1)

'It's not that life is the thing – and prayer helps you to live it: but prayer is the thing – and life allows you to express it.' (anon.)[1]

'Hands lifted in prayer must result in hands reaching out to all people with the love of God.' (George Carey)[2]

Making it happen

Prayer has a vital part to play in pastoral care – yet it can easily be neglected. This is often because people's lives are so full that finding time for quiet concentration seems impossible. An effective way of ensuring that prayer – for those in need, for those who care, for the whole life of the local church – is regularly offered is to encourage the setting up of Prayer Groups. Through belonging to a praying group people can discover that others have the same difficulties as themselves, share experiences and give each other mutual prayer support. Commitment to attending a group helps people to 'make time'.

Praying in a group

The following examples show just a few ways in which prayer groups can form part of a church's life and what they can be used for.

- 'At St Matthew's church a group meets on Saturday mornings and particularly prays for the Sunday worship. We remember those who will be leading the services. We reflect on tomorrow's readings – and the minister who is to preach often finds this helpful in preparing the sermon. We have a list of names of those for whom prayer has been asked and look for more names in the church's "prayer requests" book.'
- 'Everyone who comes to Holy Trinity is prayed for in turn – even though our membership is large. We have a group that meets regularly on a week-day evening and prays for all those on the church's roll – about 600 names, spread over a year. Two members of the group, both women, have been commissioned as "visitors". During the previous week they call on those whose names are about to come up, to find out any special concerns they have and any help they need. They invite them, if possible, to come along to the meeting at which they will be prayed for and ask them to include the members of the Prayer Group in their own prayers. Many accept this invitation and come to the group on "their" day.'
- 'A "men's breakfast", linked to our church, has recently started. A group of men meet in the Church Hall at 7.30 a.m. once a week for an hour. Over our cereal and

toast we share our concerns – and end with a time of prayer.'

Some churches encourage the forming of 'prayer partners' or 'prayer triplets'. There are many advantages in having groups that are as small as this. There are fewer practical problems about finding suitable times and places to meet; it is easier for people to 'open up'; difficulties about confidentiality are lessened.

Prayer group problems

• There is always the danger that a prayer group will become a centre for gossip. A tension exists between the desire to be personal in prayer and the importance of respecting privacy. If personal details have been given they must not be used publicly, for example in the Sunday 'intercessions', unless permission for this has been obtained. If certain information has been given in confidence, this must not be repeated outside the group.

• In time the group may feel stale. The names of the same people come up for prayer week after week, without anyone knowing whether there has been any change in their situation or their needs. It may be wise to have a 'cut-off point' after a month and to make it known that this is the group's practice. Of course, people have only to ask if they wish for prayer to continue.

• Groups sometimes become discouraged, because they do not see any results from their prayers: people who ask for prayer for healing, for example, may not seem to be healed. Such feelings of frustration and failure may stem from too narrow a view of what healing means or from a misunderstanding of the purpose of praying in a group – which is not to batter God into doing what we want, but rather to release God's healing power into people's lives so that God can do what God wants. We have to trust that prayer does bring results, even if they are not apparent to us or do not happen in our timescale or in the ways we expect. It can be helpful for a group that has become disheartened to spend some time at each meeting in recalling the good things that they are aware that God has done in their own or others' lives.

- Problems may arise out of personal irritations. Belonging to a prayer group is a great way to learn tolerance — we could say it is a 'school of love'. People often find that one person in the group grates on them, because they are repetitious, over-emotional or cold. Yet they are doing their best and need to be given, not criticism, but encouragement and help. Usually, as we get to know the irritating person better, we find that we can more readily put up with their annoying ways. As we gain in understanding, so we gain in forbearance. We may even end up by genuinely liking the person we had thought was our 'best enemy'. As with all groups, however, it is wise to build in an opportunity for review at regular intervals. This is particularly important in the case of 'partners' or 'triplets', because the relationships within a very small group are likely to be intense. If personalities continue to clash, it may be best for the group to agree to disperse — without any sense of failure — and re-form into one or more new groups.

Sustaining the practice of prayer

Continuing to pray regularly can be difficult. It may be helpful to offer people a structure to follow.

- In one church people are asked to pray for the church's concerns on a particular day of the week. They are given a prayer sheet on Sunday, listing the activities of the week, the names of those who have asked for prayer and any current concerns of the church's life. 'On Tuesdays we all try to remember to pray for each other and for our church. When Tuesday comes round it jogs our memories.'

- In another church the house groups have a similar 'rule': the members undertake to pray for each other at midday every day, if they possibly can. 'It's a habit I have got into now. Whatever I am doing at noon – at work or at home – I can send up some "arrow" prayers for the others in the group.'
- People who are housebound or even just a little less active as they get older can take part in prayer ministry. Alice is visited every Monday by someone from her church, who brings her a copy of Sunday's 'pew-sheet' and news of the church's activities and needs, as well as the needs of individuals. Alice then spends time each morning in praying for all these concerns. She is able to give time to prayer in a way that is difficult for younger people whose lives are so busy. By this means she still feels very much part of the church family and is glad that she can play a useful part in its life.
- In many churches a Prayer Board or Book is provided, where people can write their requests for prayer. These can be taken up by those who pray in the church regularly or by a prayer group.

Praying in a fellowship group

'Home groups', 'house groups', or 'fellowship groups', although they are not devoted exclusively to prayer, always include praying together as an important part of the programme. A proper amount of time – more than a few perfunctory prayers read out at the beginning and end – needs to be allotted to prayer. Some of this time may be spent in silence – with freedom for members to pray aloud as the Spirit prompts them. Thoughts arising from the group's Bible study and discussion, particular needs of members, of the local churches, of the wider community and of the world, can all be brought before God. As the group grows in its trust in God it will seem natural to turn to prayer, not only at the set 'prayer time', but at any moment. The group will place all its concerns before God and be open at all times to God's guiding voice.

Praying as a team

When a team of 'pastoral visitors' has been formed, it is helpful if, when they meet together, substantial times of prayer are included – praying for the people they care for, for the ministers and for each other.

Praying in church services

The formal 'intercessions' in the services on Sunday provide an opportunity for those who lead them to learn how to pray in public – how to put into appropriate words the desires, anxieties and aspirations of everyone present. If people find that the prayer's words match their own concerns and feelings, they will be able to join in from their hearts. If they come to church in a state of sadness or anger, they may be greatly helped by knowing that they are being prayed for.

It is useful from time to time to hold a 'workshop' on leading intercessions (as also on lesson reading) in which practical help with voice production can be given, as well as discussion of what is or is not suitable for inclusion in corporate prayers.

If the offices of Morning and Evening Prayer are said in the church at a regular time on weekdays, this provides another opportunity for people to draw from God's strength by praying together.

Praying for healing

'To be whole in body, mind and spirit is to be like Jesus. It means imitating a constant rootedness in God and his availability and love for our fellow human beings.'[3]

'From the way that healing has entered into the consciousness of many Christians, it would appear that we are witnessing a rediscovery of the enormous power and resources of the living God for the Church of our time.'[4]

In one large town, there is an ecumenical grouping of churches. Chris, who is a pastor in one of these churches, explained how they set about exploring the ministry of healing:

> We first decided we must find out more about it, so that we could be clear as to what we meant by 'healing'. We were sure that healing is far more than physical cure, but is part of God's care for the well-being of the whole person — so we warmed to the definition of healing as 'Jesus Christ meeting us at the point of our need'.[5]

> We started by forming a 'telephone prayer circle', with five churches co-operating. At first people were hesitant about joining and it was difficult to get it going, but now it means that when some special need arises, we can quickly get in touch with a large number of people who are committed to praying.

> Next we offered the laying on of hands in the regular Sunday service in one of the churches. People came forward, quietly explained what they felt was their need for healing and received ministry from a priest and his wife who are experienced in this work. Many unexpected people have responded in this way and many new opportunities for pastoral care have been opened up.

We are now starting a monthly healing service. The emphasis will be, not on seeking for 'miracles' in a narrow sense, but on prayer for wholeness.

It is good practice to offer some preparation before a healing service begins, so that people can consider such questions as:

- What do you understand by the words 'healing' and 'wholeness'?
- In what ways can healing occur?

At Iona Abbey regular healing services are held, but they are always preceded by 'a time of teaching and exploration, so that people can think about the issues and perhaps adjust their expectations.' The Iona Community supplies a 'Discussion Starter' sheet for use in small groups, to get people thinking and sharing.

Support for individual prayer life

'I would see spiritual direction, not as an off-shoot of counselling or therapy, but simply as an extension of good pastoral care.'[6]

Through the prayer life of a group people often find that their individual prayers are refreshed. But some people find they need a different kind of help: the support of a 'spiritual director' or 'soul friend'. Ministers, retreat houses and religious communities can be of great help in finding the 'right person'. In most areas help is available from someone who acts as coordinator for spiritual direction.

Always seek to do good to one another and to all. Rejoice always, pray without ceasing, give thanks in all circumstances; for this is the will of God in Christ Jesus for you.
(1 Thessalonians 4:15-18)

Story for discussion

11. Molly

TOPICS
* Seeking guidance
* Using our own experience to help others
* The church as a praying community

Molly is a committed Christian and a regular church member. She suffers from depression and has days in her life when she is unable to walk, talk, or do anything constructive. She cannot even manage to pray at these times. On good days she is an energetic and lively person. She has been praying for guidance about her future and how she can best serve God. Recently she has had the idea of working as a pastoral counsellor, as this work would be flexible. She thinks that her own experience of depression would enable her to understand and help others.

Discussion

1   How would you help Molly to find the right way forward in her life?
2   How can we test whether the ideas in our head are really our prayers being answered?
3   How can we use our own experience to help others?
4   How could the local church support Molly?

TRAINING FOR PASTORAL CARE

LEARNING TO LISTEN

Learning to make our caring more effective

As mature adults we learn in many different ways. All training should make use of the methods that are most likely to enable us to learn, taking into account the personality, gifts and experience of each individual. In this sense it should be 'learner centred'. We can learn through apprenticeship – working alongside and observing someone who is already skilled and experienced; through coaching – receiving one-to-one instruction tailored to our particular needs; through the use of self-assessment tools such as personality type indicators; through reading and listening and applying what we read and hear.

We learn also through reflecting on our own experience – a practice that helps us to act more wisely in the future and is often enhanced by attending courses using 'experiential' methods.

All these methods are complementary to each other. Learning events such as courses and workshops are important because they enable members to work in small groups, to take part in practical exercises and, by sharing ideas and experiences, to learn from and energize each other. A course can encourage members to value what they already know, introduce them to new ideas, assist them in developing skills, point them to resources they can draw on (both outside and within themselves), and help them to find renewed confidence in God's guiding of their lives.

This chapter contains:

- Advice on planning a course – practical suggestions.
- Details of a basic course – full description of a course that encourages members to reflect on their own experience.

Planning a course

When it has been decided to provide a basic course in Pastoral Care for members of your church, start by convening a small planning group of about five people. It will need to meet several times, to cover the following agenda:

- Clarify the overall aim of the course. It is a useful discipline to express this aim in a single sentence, which might be something like this: 'To enable those who join the course to become more confident and skilled in offering friendly support to their neighbours, particularly at times of special need.'
- Identify the specific objectives of the course – which might be along the following lines.

To help participants to:
1 Understand what 'pastoral care' means:
   - how it flows from our commitment as disciples of Jesus Christ;
   - how it differs from the friendly care that anyone might give;
   - the activities it includes;
   - the problems and dangers it may involve;
   - the rewards it may bring.

2 Understand their own:
   - practice of pastoral care;
   - motives;
   - strengths, weaknesses, gifts, difficulties.
3 Observe and reflect on how people around them behave.
4 Understand how people interact and relate.
5 Develop their 'pastoral skills'.

- Consider what resources are available from outside. A number of organizations produce useful material and run local events.[1] Or your diocese or central training department may provide an appropriate course. Alternatively, you may decide to devise your own course, drawing for help on some of these outside resources, as well as on experienced people in your local community.
- Agree on a title for the course, and work out a timetable and programme. Decide how many sessions you want to have and how the subject is to be divided up between them.
- Consider who is to be the overall leader of the course – to introduce and facilitate the sessions and to give the course its particular 'flavour'.
- Consider who is to be responsible for administration – for keeping everyone informed, typing and photocopying hand-outs, making sure that everything needed is available. It is preferable for the course leader to be relieved of these tasks.

Note: These decisions about people are crucial and should not be hurried. The 'obvious' people may or may not be the right ones to take these roles. People need to be found who have appropriate skills and experience.

- Consider if it would be useful to bring in other people to lead specific sections of the course. Are there people locally who could contribute valuable experience? For example, there may be a community nurse who could talk about

coping with illness or about post-natal depression, or a
member of your congregation who is a trained counsellor
and could lead a session on listening skills.
• There will be practical matters to be settled, including:

1 Place and time.
2 The best size for the group.
3 How to recruit people to join the course.
4 What publicity will be needed.
5 What costs will be incurred and how they will be paid
   for – these may include the costs of: renting a place
   to meet, printing of posters and leaflets, stationery,
   photocopying, postage, telephone, refreshments, travel
   expenses and/or a fee, if visiting speakers are used.

Designing the course sessions

At the stage when all the above matters have been settled and it
is known who will be joining the course, make a detailed design
for each session.

• Again, begin by clarifying aims: write down exactly what you
  hope to achieve in each session.
• Make a draft of the plan for the first session, with as much
  detail as possible and realistic timings.
• Consider the methods you want to use. In order to make the
  sessions enjoyable, practical and memorable, you will need
  to use a variety of methods. Most people learn best when
  they are actively involved: active, participatory methods
  should therefore be used whenever possible – although there
  will also be times when it will be appropriate to give a
  'talk'. Some active methods you might consider are given
  in Chapter 12.

There follows a full description of a basic course, entitled 'Listening and Caring', that has been run successfully in several
local churches. It offers a starting point, rather than a blueprint,

for those who wish to design their own training events. Brief outlines of two follow-on courses, for those who want to explore further, are included in Chapter 12.

'Listening and caring'

This course was first held in the home of Pamela, with Brian as leader and 17 other members. The four sessions ran weekly, on weekday mornings from 10.00 a.m. to 12.00 noon.

Aim
To enable those who join the course to become more confident and skilled in offering friendly support to their neighbours, as part of their Christian discipleship, especially through effective listening.

Session 1	Better listening
Session 2	Why do we care?
Session 3	Christian caring
Session 4	Looking forward

Points for the leader
- Remember that this is an introductory course, which is not primarily intended to convey information. Rather it attempts to stimulate members to reflect on the meaning of 'pastoral care' and on issues that arise in relation to caring, and to help them to develop their skills.
- Be aware of the needs and abilities of course members, in order to make sure that they can benefit fully from the course. There may be a wide range of ability, so keep any 'input' simple and clear. Bear in mind the needs of people who find it hard to express themselves in words or find reading difficult.
- Notice that 'listening skills' are a key element of the course. Make it clear that these are not the same as, though they are included in, 'counselling skills'.

- Encourage course members to care for each other. An
effective way of doing this is to form them into 'pastoral
groups', with three or four people in each. Then, if
members can arrive a little early, these groups can sit
together before the session begins, catch up with each
other's lives and pray together. They can also pray for each
other during the week.

Session 1 – Better listening

Aim
To consider why listening is important and how we can learn to
listen better.

For the leader to do beforehand
- Prepare handouts:
  - list of names and addresses of course members
  - suggestions for homework
  - 'Good Listening' (see Chapter 12)
- Copy the plan for Session 1 on to a large sheet of paper.
- Check that a flip-chart, pad and pens will be available.
- Arrange for someone to be responsible for providing
refreshments throughout the course and decide how these
will be paid for. (Either make a fixed charge or ask for
contributions or pay for them out of church funds.)
- Decide what method will be used to get members into
groups of three for the 'Listening Exercise'. (See suggestions
in Chapter 12.)
- Consider what prayers are to be used near the beginning and
at the end of the session. (For the later sessions a course
member might be asked to lead them.)

PROGRAMME
10.00 a.m. Introduction
Welcome.

Introductions — of leader and members.

Thanks to Pamela for lending her house for the meetings.

Reasons for running the course and its aims and objectives.

Emphasis on the responsibility of members themselves to make the most of what is offered in the course: by reflecting on what happens and especially by doing the suggested 'homework' between sessions; by keeping a notebook or journal; by meeting with others for support and prayer.

Outline the programme for the four sessions of the course.

Describe the methods that will be used: not listening to lectures, but learning by doing.

Explain the basic assumptions of the course:

1   The sharing of neighbourly pastoral care is central
    to our Christian commitment.
2   We want to increase our skills and we believe this
    is possible.
3   We are all at different stages and have different gifts,
    but we respect, trust and care for each other.
4   Confidentiality is important — anything said by members
    during course sessions must not be repeated elsewhere
    without permission.

Outline the plan for today's session. (It is useful to have this plan, with timings, written on a large sheet of paper and put up on the wall, so that everyone knows 'where we are going'.)

Opportunity for comments or questions.

Time of prayer. (A time of prayer is often most helpful if it is
not placed right at the beginning, but at a later point when
members have had a chance to get their bearings.)

10.30 a.m. First activity – getting to know each other
The leader explains that one way of learning about caring is for
members to become a caring group themselves. So the session
starts with an activity aimed at helping them to get to know
each other better. (The exact form of this exercise will depend
on whether members already know each other well.)

Members are asked to stand up and form a circle, getting into
alphabetical order according to their first names. Everyone then
has a few minutes for chatting with the people next to them.
They might share: whether they like or dislike their name; why
they have joined the course; how they are feeling now. (If there
is time, or as an alternative, this could be repeated with everyone standing in order of surnames or in height order.)

People return to their seats and discuss, all together, how they
felt during the activity. Did they have strong feelings about their
names, in relation to their own sense of identity? How could we
be sensitive to others who might suffer from feeling invisible,
marginalized or stereotyped?

10.45 a.m. Second activity – a listening exercise
Form members into groups of three.

Suggest that everyone makes sure they know each other's names
and a little about each other.

The groups then decide who, in their 'three', will take the
following roles: 'talker', 'listener', 'observer/timekeeper'. The
'talkers' are then to talk, for about ten minutes, about something

they genuinely want to talk about. It might be something that has recently happened, something they feel strongly about, are worried about – or are particularly happy about. The 'listeners' are to listen as helpfully as possible, asking brief questions or giving sympathetic prompts as necessary. The 'observers' are to watch the other two, particularly noticing 'body language' – tone of voice, gestures, pauses.

After about 10 minutes the 'observers' stop the talkers, and the groups spend 15 minutes exploring what has been happening. What did each person in turn notice and how did they feel? What did the 'observers' observe?'

11.15 a.m. In the full group – feedback and discussion

Ask for observations both on the last exercise and on the whole session so far. (During this time people will produce valuable insights about 'listening' which should be recorded briefly on the flip-chart. These should be typed up afterwards and given out at the next session.)

11.45 a.m. Give out homework

- Read hand-out on 'Good Listening'.
- Think about what happened in the session, especially in the 'listening' exercise. Did any new questions arise for you?
- Recall some occasion when you listened to someone else. What did you gain from doing this?
- Do you think that looking at Jesus's example helps us to understand why and how we should care for others? What, if anything, do you think is special about Christian caring?
- Notice whether anything in the worship in church next Sunday illuminates any of these questions for you.

11.50–12.00 noon. Time of prayer

Include 'open prayer': for those in the local community who are known to be in special need – and for members of the course and of the church. End by standing in a circle, holding hands, to say 'the Grace'.

* Note for leader: Ask someone else to lead the opening prayers next time.

Session 2 – Why do we care?

Aim
To consider what we mean by 'caring' and why we want to do it.

For the leader to do beforehand
* Prepare handouts:
  - comments from flip-chart from previous session
  - story: *Diana and Henry* (see below)
  - suggestions for homework
  - 'Our motives for caring' (see Chapter 12)
* Copy plan for Session 2 on to a large sheet of paper.
* Check that a flip-chart, pad and pens will be available.
* Consider the prayers and who will lead them.
* Make a list for yourself of points about 'the characteristics of caring' – to be fed in to the discussion if necessary.

PROGRAMME
10.00 a.m. Introduction
Prayers.

Outline of the plan for today's session.

Give out feedback comments from last time and allow a few minutes to read them.

'Recap' of last time and review of homework.

10.30 a.m. What do we mean by 'caring'?

Brainstorm: what have you recently done in your church, community, workplace or home that you think of as 'caring' activities? (Someone writes all the suggestions on the flip-chart.)

Plenary discussion: looking at those activities, what do you think are the characteristics of 'caring'? (Make notes of people's ideas on the flip-chart. The leader should make a list of the important points in advance. Then a little prompting can be done if something vital is omitted. See end of this session, for points made by Brian's group.)

11.00 a.m. Exercise – Why do we 'care'?

To explore our motivation, using the story of *Diana and Henry* (see p. 206). Either read out the story or give everyone a copy and allow time to read it – and to think about the situation in the story on their own for a few minutes. Then form small groups of two or three and consider the questions that follow the story.

11.20 a.m. Discussion in the full group

Ask for brief responses to the story.

Then concentrate on the third question – about Diana's motives, conscious and unconscious – noting suggestions on the flip-chart.

11.45 a.m. Feedback and homework

Ask for reactions to the session as a whole. If there are worries or questions that cannot be dealt with properly at this point, they should be noted so that they can be returned to later.

Give out homework:
• Read hand-out on 'Our motives for caring'.
• Think over Session 2. What questions were raised for you? Did you learn anything new?

- Using incidents in your experience this week, continue to observe what it means to care for someone, why people care, why you care and how this caring is carried out.
- Read the 'Beatitudes' (Matthew 5:1–14) and consider whether, and in what ways, Christ's teaching in this passage affects your daily life.

11.50 a.m. Time of prayer
Ending with the Grace as before – or in some other way – to finish at 12.00 noon.

Points made by Brian's group during Session 2
Caring:
- Can be carried out by anyone.
- Involves giving our time, our love, ourselves. (But how can we best use our own experience to help someone else?)
- Is concerned with individuals. (But should it also aim to change society?)
- Is mostly carried out by individuals, but also by a group, community or 'society'.
- Is not the same as 'counselling', though both involve 'listening'.
- Is not the same as professional help, but may involve knowing when to suggest this.
- Springs out of concern and love, but also from many other motives.
- Requires self-awareness: of motives and rewards for oneself; of own skills and non-skills and what one could learn, or not; of own assumptions and prejudices.
- Often involves taking a risk: of upsetting someone or of being rebuffed.
- Is sometimes prompted at first by conscience, but then leads to love: 'ought' turns into 'want'.
- Is often focused on problems – but not invariably.
- Can consist of practical help, giving advice, listening, sharing our faith, just being there ... usually a mixture of these.

Why does one person want to help another person?

Some reasons that Pamela's group thought of in relation to the story of 'Diana and Henry':

- She cares about him.
- She feels a bond of Christian fellowship with him.
- She wants to make other people happy, especially people she loves.
- She wants Henry to make good decisions in future and she thinks she knows what he ought to do now.
- She sees herself as a rescuer.
- She feels responsible; she feels it has to be *her*.
- She feels guilty that she did not help more in the past.
- She feels empathy – she thinks she can identify with Henry.
- She feels frustrated by Henry's mistakes and muddles.
- She is projecting her own problems on to Henry, such as her own frustrations with life generally.
- She has a sense of superiority over Henry, which she might lose if she cannot help him.
- She feels disappointed by the situation Henry has got into. She had hoped he would make a successful marriage and would bring his wife to Christ.
- She had helped him in the past, so she needs the satisfaction of feeling that she can still help him, that he is still dependent on her.
- She suspects that he needs professional help and wants to arrange this.
- She wants to help him to see his situation more clearly.
- She wants to witness to God's love and forgiveness, through giving help to others.
- She needs to be needed – to be important to Henry.

In conclusion Pamela quoted: '*I will give you all the care that I need!*' stressing that our motives are always mixed. It is important that we should become aware of them.

Session 3 – Christian caring

Aim
To consider what is distinctive about Christian caring in the light of Jesus's teaching and practice.

For the leader to do beforehand
* Prepare handouts:
  – comments from flip-chart from previous session
  – Bible passages (Matthew 5:1–14; Luke 8:40–56) and questions, for 1st and 2nd Exercises (see below)
  – suggestions for homework
  – 'Christian caring' and/or 'A ministry of wholeness' (see Chapter 12)
* Copy plan for Session 3 on to large sheet of paper.
* Check that a flip-chart, pad and pens will be available.
* Check that large sheets of paper and thick pens will be available for use by the small groups. Also Blu-Tack or drawing pins, if appropriate.
* Consider the prayers and who will lead them.

PROGRAMME
10.00 a.m. Introduction
Prayers.

Give out the feedback comments from last time and allow a few minutes for members to read them.

'Recap' of last session and review of homework.

Outline the plan for today's session.

10.30 a.m. First Exercise – to look at Jesus's teaching
Read out the 'Beatitudes': Matthew 5:1–14 and then give out copies of it – so that everyone is using the same version.

Form members into groups of three.

Ask them to discuss for ten minutes: 'Does this teaching by Jesus say anything to us about why and how we should care for each other?'

Return to the full group, ask for suggestions and write them up on the flip-chart.

11.00 a.m. Second Exercise – to look at how Jesus himself cared for people
First, with everyone together, read out the story about Jesus in Luke 8:40–56.

Get them into small groups of three or four and give out copies of the story and questions.

Supply each group with a large sheet of paper and thick pen.

Ask them each to choose one of the characters in the story and to identify themselves with that character as they listen to the story again: either the woman or Jairus or Peter or Jesus. Each member of a small group should take a different role.

One member of each group reads the story aloud again quite slowly. As members listen, they should see and feel all that happens from the point of view of the person whose role they have taken.

Then, remaining in their roles, take fifteen minutes to talk about the following questions:

• What were your needs?
• What did you expect?
• What happened and what did you feel at the time?
• What did you feel afterwards?

Ask everyone to come out of role, remain in small groups and take fifteen minutes to consider:

- Has anything so far thrown light on why and how we should 'care'?
- How do these points relate to your own feelings and attitudes?

The groups should choose the two or three most important of their observations and write them on a large sheet of paper.

In the full group: Put the sheets of paper up on the wall (or if this is not possible spread them on the floor) and allow time (about fifteen minutes) for members to read them. Ask if anyone wishes to comment on any of these observations or to make any other point. All the points made should be typed up afterwards and given out at the next session. (See below for ideas from Brian's group.)

11.45 a.m. Give out homework
- Read handout on 'Christian caring' and/or 'A ministry of wholeness'.
- Think back over the last Session and make a note of any new insights or any questions you would like to explore further in the future.
- Consider doing the Second Exercise again in some other setting – perhaps in a house group or with your family or a friend – either using the same passage or a different one.
- Look for connections between what you read in the Bible or say and hear in church and what happens in your life this week, including your encounters with other people.
- Consider: when is it most helpful for 'caring' to be offered by you as an individual, by the local church, by some other person or group, or by 'society' in some form?

11.50 a.m. Time of prayer
As before.

Ideas and further questions from Brian's group

- Jesus cared equally for the President of the Synagogue and for an unknown woman: he made no difference for social position or gender. Who, in our society, would be in equivalent positions, one powerful, the other low in the social scale and despised by others?

- There had to be faith on the part of the sufferer or someone else. Therefore in any situation of need we – who have faith – must always pray, entrusting the other person to God's care.

- Jesus was calm, even when everyone around him was rocked by strong emotions. What kind of calm did Jesus have and how can we learn to have it too?

- Sometimes a person only finds faith when they reach a point of desperation and become willing to ask for help. How can we be strong and confident and yet show people that this comes from accepting our dependence on God? How can we help another person to let go and trust God?

- Peter tried to protect Jesus. Perhaps he was right to do so, because 'carers' also need to be cared for. But perhaps his motive was partly selfish – he wanted Jesus to be available for *him* and not to be drained by the demands of others. When we try to protect someone, are we sure it is really in that person's best interests? Have we, as carers, got proper support?

Session 4 – Looking forward

Aims
To explore further a number of issues about pastoral care, including questions raised by course members.

To assist members in drawing up personal guidelines for their future caring ministry in the church.

For the leader to do beforehand

- Prepare handouts:
  - comments from flip-chart from previous session
  - *Tessa and Marianne* − story and exercise in four parts (see pp. 207–8). Print enough copies for everyone. Each of the four parts must be printed separately, so that they can be given out in succession as the next part of the exercise is reached.
  - suggestions for final homework
  - 'Boundaries' (see Chapter 12)
  - evaluation sheet (see samples in Chapter 12)
- Copy plan for Session 4 on to a large sheet of paper.
- Check that a flip-chart, pad and pens will be available.
- Consider the prayers and who will lead them.

PROGRAMME
10.00 a.m. Introduction
Prayers.

Give out the feedback comments from last time and allow a few minutes for members to read them.

'Recap' of last session and review of homework.

Outline the plan for today's session.

10.20 a.m. Exercise − to explore issues about 'boundaries', using the story of *Tessa and Marianne* (see pp. 207–8).
Get members into small groups of three or four and work through the four parts of the exercise.

Return to the full group. Ask if members want to make any comments about today's exercise or about anything else that has arisen during the course (15 minutes).

11.15 a.m. Personal guidelines
Ask for suggestions for personal guidelines for pastoral care.

Write up all ideas on flip-chart, discussing them with the group as you do so.

11.30 a.m. The future
Get into pairs to talk about 'your future role in the church' (five or six minutes for each person).

- Now that you have done the course, will your role be any different from before?
- In what ways do you think your own understanding and skills have increased?

11.45 a.m. Feedback
Do a round, asking each member to say, in a few sentences, what they have gained from the course and what they are feeling now.

Stress that this has been an introductory course, drawing attention to some of the important topics that have not been covered in this course, such as 'loss and bereavement'.

Give out 'Boundaries' and evaluation sheets. Ask members if possible to fill in the sheets before they leave.

Give out final homework:
- If you have not already done so, fill in the evaluation sheet.
- Try to take some time to think out and write down your answers to the following:
  - What will it involve for you to become a more Christ-like carer?
  - How will you develop your own self-understanding in future?
  - What are your own needs for care at the moment?

11.55 a.m. Time of prayer.

- Note for leader: a final hand-out should be produced from today's flip-chart notes.

Diana and Henry

Henry is a retired man in his late sixties who used to be active in St Martin's Church. He lost his wife ten years ago. Diana and James, who are married to each other, are also active members of the church. They got to know Henry quite well through working together on various church activities. Henry confided to them how lonely he felt and how much he would like to get married again.

Early last year Henry's married daughter persuaded him to move to a 'retirement flat' in her area, about 25 miles away from his former home. One day he rang James and Diana up: 'I've got some wonderful news! I'm getting married!' His fiancee, Joan, was a single lady, about his age, who lived in a flat in the same block. They had first met each other in the communal lounge. They were planning to be married in church, although unfortunately Joan wasn't a Christian. They would live in Joan's flat, as it was slightly bigger — and when they got round to it they would sell Henry's. 'Isn't it all rather quick?' Diana asked — she knew him well enough to be frank. 'Yes, I suppose it is,' he replied, 'but we get on so well, I feel sure it will be all right.' They married last July and their friends believed they had settled down happily.

Last week Diana happened to be in the area where Henry now lives, so she dropped in to see him. She found him in his old flat. He did not seem his usual cheery self and there was no sign of Joan. It soon came out that they had been having problems. For example Joan had not liked it when Henry wanted to move a lot of his possessions into her flat. She had also been unwilling to change her set routine. (Of course, Diana realized that she was only hearing Henry's side of the story.) So they had decided to go back to living in their separate flats for the time being. 'We are getting on better now ... we are good friends, but I don't feel as if I am married,' Henry said sadly, 'I am afraid it has all been a big mistake.'

Diana could not stay any longer that afternoon, but for the last few days she has been feeling concerned about Henry. She has been wondering what to do. She would really like to help Henry.

QUESTIONS
• Should Diana do anything?
• What do you suggest she might do?
• What are Diana's motives in wanting to help Henry?

Tessa and Marianne – Part 1 (5 minutes)
Everyone reads the story below to themselves.

Tessa is an active member of her church. Some months ago she was rung up by a clergyman in a neighbouring area, the Rev. Kevin Keene, whom she knows, asking her to befriend a young woman called Marianne, who has been an occasional member of his congregation. He explained that Marianne had made a late marriage at the age of 38, but it had only lasted two years and had now broken up. Marianne had returned to live with her mother, a widow called Edna, who lives in the same village as Tessa. Edna comes regularly to church and Tessa knows her slightly.

Tessa rings up Marianne and invites her to come round to her house for a cup of tea the next afternoon. Marianne pours out the story of her marriage – and her present unhappiness – and also much about her former life and work. It is a long story and Tessa does not do much except ask occasional questions. She surreptitiously looks at her watch and realizes it is now time to prepare the evening meal for her family.

In groups, decide who will take the roles of Tessa and Marianne. Others should act as observers. If necessary read the story again. 'Tessa' and 'Marianne' continue the conversation briefly until Marianne leaves.

Tessa and Marianne – Part 2 (5 minutes)
Decide who will take the role of Edna. Everyone reads the next part of the story to themselves.

It is now several weeks later and Marianne has had several further lengthy chats with Tessa, going over her disastrous marriage and its ending and the difficult position she is now in. She hates having to live with her mother, with so little privacy. But there is no hope of reconciliation and, until the divorce is settled, she has almost no money.

One day Edna catches Tessa after church and tells her that she is hurt that Marianne doesn't confide in her and doesn't want to come with her to church. 'It's all so difficult,' she says and asks Tessa to come round to see her. Tessa is uneasy about this, but feels she must accept. When she gets there she discovers that Marianne is out and that Edna has kept the visit secret from her, which increases Tessa's sense of unease. She lets Edna talk, but leaves as soon as she can.

'Tessa' and 'Edna' continue the conversation until Tessa leaves (5 minutes).

Tessa and Marianne – Part 3 (up to 15 minutes)
Decide who will take the role of the Rev. Kevin Keane.

The next day Tessa goes to see Kevin.

'Tessa' and 'Kevin' have a conversation about Marianne, in order to help Tessa to handle the situation when she sees Marianne again.

Tessa and Marianne – Part 4 (15–20 minutes)
Tell everyone to come out of role.

Then, still in the small groups, explore together:

• What are the main issues raised by this story?
• Could Tessa have handled things differently or better? If so, how?
• How might Tessa's Christian faith help the situation?
• Could the church help? A minister? The congregation? A smaller group within it?

AIDS TO LEARNING

This chapter contains:

- Active methods and exercises – list with explanations
- List of stories and discussion topics
- Hand-outs to go with the course outlined in the previous
  chapter – for members to keep for reference
  1 Good listening
  2 Our motives for caring
  3 Christian caring
  4 A ministry of wholeness
  5 Boundaries
- More courses – outline programmes of two follow-on courses
- Evaluation – samples of 'evaluation sheets'

Active training methods

Here are some active exercises to use with a group of up to twenty people.

- **Using an ice-breaker** at the beginning of the session. Useful both to help people to relax and to get to know each other. (An example is given in Session 1 of the basic course in Chapter 11.)
- **Brainstorming.** Ask members to call out any words or ideas that come to them. All suggestions are recorded on the flip-chart and no discussion is allowed at this stage. When the page is full, the process stops and discussion then takes place. A technique that often produces valuable insights, useful practical ideas or a new slant on an issue.
- **Doing a round.** Go round the group asking each member in turn to give a brief answer to a question. Examples: 'In one word, how are you feeling now?' ... 'What do you hope to gain from this course?' ... 'What does the word training (or healing or leadership or confession) suggest to you?' Useful when a quick impression is needed of how members are feeling or how they react to a particular concept.
- **Role play.** Each member of a small group takes on a 'part' or 'role', identifies with, and speaks from the point of view of, that person. At the end, members must be given an opportunity consciously to 'come out of role'. People often react against the idea of doing 'role play', because they think they will have to 'act'. They should be reassured that they will only be asked to 'talk' and that it is worth trying because the insights gained through this method are so valuable. Perhaps the use of the term 'role play' can be avoided!
- **Breaking into small groups** for an activity or discussion. Plan in advance how these groups will be formed. It can feel daunting simply to be told to 'get into groups', especially at the beginning of a course. Possible ways to do this include:

Use a 'numbering' method: go round the circle giving each
person a number and then ask those with the same number
to form a group. With a group of eighteen people,
numbering up to three will produce three groups of six
or numbering up to six will produce six groups of three.
Write numbers on slips of paper and put them into a 'hat'
to pass round: the number picked tells you which group
to join.

Work out suitable groupings yourself in advance.

- **Using buzz groups.** Ask members to turn to the person
next to them and have a brief discussion – for two or three
minutes only – of a question they have been given. Helps
people to relax and gets their minds going on a subject. This
can help forward any plenary discussion that may follow.
- **Using someone as an observer** during an activity and
then listening to and discussing that person's comments.
- **Looking at a key Bible passage** (such as the 'Beatitudes'
– Matthew 5:1–10) or a section of the liturgy (such as one of
the Creeds) and considering in what ways it might influence
how we view other people and behave towards them.
- **Telling stories.** Using a story – a case history or imaginary
scenario – as a starter for a discussion. Stories can stimulate
us to think about human relationships. By entering into
stories and reflecting on them, we can develop our ability
to empathize with and encourage each other. Discussion is
more productive when it is based on stories from 'real life'
– which may be 'untidy', but carry conviction – rather than
on invented scenarios. Below is a list of the stories attached
to earlier chapters, together with the most important issues
raised in each.

Stories and discussion topics

1. Carol and Madeleine (Chapter 1)
- Caring for the whole person
- Sharing our faith
- The need for training
- Discerning when professional help is needed
- How much time should I give?
- Letting go

2. Tracy, Mandy, Martha and Jack (Chapter 2)
- Moral principles
- Speaking frankly

3. Pauline, John, Susan and Nic (Chapter 2)
- Boundaries
  - how can I balance family, job and caring for others?
  - can a professional relationship be a friendly one as well?
- Being truthful
- Step-parents and step-children

4. Simon (Chapter 3)
- Care for the whole person
- Community action
- Pastoral care and evangelism
- Motives

5. Doreen (Chapter 4)
- Issues for Christians at work
- Support by the church
- Doing theology

6. Duncan (Chapter 5)
- Support by the church family
- Can ministers help?
- Giving advice
- Responding to people's needs

7. Viv, Len, Toni and Gillian (Chapter 6)
• Support by the church
• Listening
• Family relationships
• Parents and teenagers

8. Graham, Angie and Dawn (Chapter 7)
• Strains on a marriage
• Getting involved
• Conflicting demands

9. Shirley, Clive, Peter and Helen (Chapter 8)
• Baptism
• Having doubts
• Conflicting feelings
• The role of a minister

10. Peggy, Jim and Jennifer (Chapter 8)
• Support by the church family
• Values
• Parents and teenagers

11. Molly (Chapter 10)
• Seeking guidance
• Using our own experience to help others
• The church as a praying community

Hand-outs

Busy people today, even if they enjoy reading, do not often have time to read books. Many of us feel we do a daily battle with the torrent of paper that flows into our homes, trying to read, absorb, sift and store it. Our pastoral care for course members (especially a course in 'Pastoral Care') should avoid overburdening them with booklists and making them feel guilty if they cannot do much reading.

But 'hand-outs', which summarize what they have learned and which they can keep for reference – especially if they are clearly written in 'plain English' – are essential aids and greatly appreciated. Five examples follow – which supplement the 'Listening and Caring' course.

For Session 1 GOOD LISTENING

'It was not what she said, but her acceptance of me that counted.' (From a newspaper article)

'People resolve their own problems one way or another – I just listen while they are doing it.' (From an article by a member of the Samaritans)

'I am sure you believe you understand what you think I said, but I'm not sure you realise that what you heard is not what I meant.' (On the wall of a psychiatrist's room)

'To listen is not a passive affair, but a conscious, willed action, requiring alertness and vigilance, by which our whole attention is focused and controlled.' (Mother Mary Clare)

We all do a lot of listening.

When?
• In meetings – of all kinds: committees and other small groups; large groups; church services.
• When we receive formal instruction, such as a lecture or sermon.
• In casual situations – at home, at work, waiting at the school gate, over coffee after church.
• In situations where we find ourselves in an informal counselling role: we visit someone who is depressed or a friend starts talking about her problems in her marriage.

Why?
Good listening means hearing what is really being said, instead of half-hearing or mishearing. Good listening is important because through it we can:

- learn a great deal for our own benefit;
- make well-informed decisions;
- help people who need to talk;
- get on better with the other people in our lives;
- show love and respect for another person, reflecting God's love.

Christ-like love consists, not primarily in doing something 'for' or 'to' another person, but in standing 'with' them – which often means listening.

How?
Good listening is often prevented by:
- being in a hurry;
- having one's mind full of other concerns;
- not taking the other person seriously: not caring/not really being interested/not believing that what they are saying is important;
- having preconceived ideas as to what the other person will say/jumping to hasty conclusions/falling for hasty impressions;
- our own need to talk about our own concerns and experience – which are rarely helpful to the other person;
- offering advice or solutions or stories of similar experiences of our own – which may boost our own morale but are rarely felt by the other person to be appropriate;
- our own beliefs and moral code; our feelings of disapproval or judgement; our lack of respect for other people's right to work out their own moral conduct;
- our own feelings of guilt and the urge to justify ourselves;
- our own hang-ups, memories, prejudices, strong feelings – we may be afraid of being hurt by these, especially if we don't understand them well enough;
- finding the other person unattractive, stupid, slow or boring;
- feelings of embarrassment if there is a silence or if the other person cries or shows strong feelings;

- fear of getting more involved than one had bargained for; of getting into deep water and not being able to cope;
- trying to 'do good' – because often this is a way of satisfying our own need for power, self-esteem or approval; but if we really care and listen with understanding, then 'good' is sure to emerge – but as a by-product.

Good listening can be helped by:

- slowing ourselves down;
- trying to *understand* – while accepting that one can never fully understand another person; offering 'empathy': 'standing beside' the other person;
- getting into the habit of noticing body language and remarks dropped out casually – and discerning their significance;
- listening for the *feelings* that *lie behind* a person's words and body language;
- accepting these and showing empathy by 'reflecting back' – but if one is not sure, it may be better not to say anything for a while, rather than get it wrong;
- taking other people seriously: respecting their opinions; accepting them personally, even if they do not appear attractive; being genuine in one's caring;
- trying to see the person within the whole context of their life, not just in the circumstances of this incident;
- focusing on the *person*, rather than the *problem* – the *person* who is talking to me and needing help; remembering that a problem does not exist independently of the person who has it;
- resisting the urge to fill silences by asking questions; but also noticing if the other person needs help in putting feelings into words – one might say, 'It is difficult sometimes to find words for our feelings, isn't it?'
- helping another person to summon up their own strengths to analyse and cope with the situation themselves;
- listening for *what is going on* (sometimes referred to as the 'transaction' or 'process'):

  – between the other person and oneself;
  – between the other person and spouse, relatives, friends;
  – between several people in a group;
- noticing our own feelings while we listen: asking ourselves: 'what effect is this person having on *me*?'
- making sure that we have someone else 'who will to listen to *me*' – someone to help us to 'unload' and to become more aware of our own motives, hang-ups, emotions, preconceived ideas, moral code and defensiveness.

How Long?

You will have to decide how long to go on listening: on any one occasion and on how many occasions. Making a person dependent or over protected does not help them in the long run. You – and your family – have *your* needs too, which should be respected.

There are times when it is not a good idea to do any prolonged listening yourself: when it is better to refer the person to someone else or find some other way of dealing with the situation. Be careful not to be carried away by your own desire to be seen as a sympathetic person. Yet sometimes we need to 'take a risk'. We can do this if, through prayer, we are looking at the situation in the light of God's love.

For Session 2 OUR MOTIVES FOR CARING

'You shall love your neighbour as yourself.' (Leviticus 19:18)

Motivation and rewards – the 'feel-good' factor

'He [a lawyer] asked Jesus: 'And who is my neighbour?' (Luke 10:29). Jesus answered the question by telling the story that we refer to as 'The Good Samaritan'. In doing so he neatly switched the viewpoint from that of a person who is primarily the receiver of care, to that of someone who actively delivers care: 'Which of these three, do you think, was a neighbour to the man who fell into the hands of robbers?' (Luke 10:36). We are always 'neighbour' in both modes. As well as giving, we always receive rewards. 'Caring' always brings mutual benefits – it is a mutual process.

There is no harm in 'receiving' rewards. We are, after all, commanded to love our neighbours, not *without a thought for ourselves*, but *as ourselves*. Yet we do need to be aware of what is going on. Everyone should take an honest look at their motives from time to time, so that they can understand what form their 'self-love' is taking. A knowledge of basic psychology can help.

We are all prone to deceive ourselves. People may think they are 'taking up their cross' when they help someone else, but they may also be getting satisfaction from their weekly visits to an exhausted mother, from being asked for advice on their friends' tangled relationships or from patiently giving support to members of their own family.

Caring is *a mutual process*: this means that everyone can be both a giver and receiver of care. There are many housebound or elderly people who cannot rush round with meals, look after children or weed gardens, but they do a great deal to help others by being faithful in prayer. And simply by being cheerful, understanding and encouraging to the neighbour who comes to help them, they are ensuring that 'care' is *exchanged* and is truly mutual.

Dorothy is an elderly lady who used to grumble about her dependent and demanding husband, to whose needs she had to give all her time and energy. Then he died suddenly from a heart attack and, far from being relieved, Dorothy was devastated — because she was not needed any more. It was all that hard work in looking after him that had given focus to her daily round. For all his tiresome ways, he had made her life worthwhile.

When Michael goes to visit Arthur, who is lonely and housebound, Arthur benefits from Michael's company, but Michael also benefits:

- He *enjoys* Arthur's company.
- He *learns* something from the experience.
- He feels *pleased that he is needed*.
- He feels *satisfaction* that he has made the visit and carried it out sensitively and cheerfully: that he has done a good job.

Michael offers Arthur his time and his friendship. Arthur gives him friendship too, but his *chief gift* to Michael is *his need*.

Yet there are also those who, at a particular time, are sunk so deep in their own troubles that they cannot even 'see' anyone else. They have a great need to *receive* care, but, for the moment, they are not capable of *giving care* to others.

For Session 3 CHRISTIAN CARING

Some characteristics of 'Christian care'
• 'Caring' is part of the **commitment** of Christians. As
  disciples of Jesus, they follow his call, his teaching about
  God's love and his example. 'Just as I have loved you, you
  also should love one another' (John 13:34).
• Christians are **sustained** in their caring by trusting that
  God is with them to strengthen them. 'The immeasurable
  greatness of his power for us who believe' (Ephesians 1:19).
• Christians have a particular **motive** for caring: to make the
  love of Jesus known to all people. 'By this everyone will
  know that you are my disciples, if you have love for one
  another' (John 13:35).
• As followers of Jesus, Christians believe that they themselves
  are being **transformed** into new people, whose very nature
  is to love as Jesus loves. 'Let your bearing towards one
  another arise out of your life in Christ Jesus' (Philippians 2:5
  New English Bible).
• The care offered by Christians has a special **quality**, because
  it is not only 'caring for', but also 'caring about', whole
  people – and God's purpose for their lives. 'When Jesus saw
  their faith, he said to the paralytic, "Son, your sins are
  forgiven."' (Mark 2:5).
• Christians are **guided by the Holy Spirit** as to what they
  should do and how they should do it. 'When the Spirit of
  truth comes, he will guide you into all the truth' (John 16:13).

Some images that that have been used to describe a Christian
carer:
• The good shepherd
• The wounded healer
• The wise fool[1]

Pastoral care has these functions:
- Healing
- Sustaining
- Guiding
- Reconciling

Caring always brings mutual benefits.

Every human activity has a 'caring' aspect.

Caring involves everyone – not just the vicar, minister, elders or authorized pastoral visitors. We are all called to care for each other and this is the most important mark of a truly Christ-like community.

Caring is corporate as well as individual. This means that caring can sometimes be done best:
- by means of a group effort;
- by putting pressure on statutory bodies;
- by being politically active – through campaigning to improve the conditions of people's lives.

For Session 3 A MINISTRY OF WHOLENESS

As Christians involved in pastoral care we wish for the person's good at the level of the whole person. We use the concept of 'wholeness' in several senses:

WE MINISTER TO THE WHOLE OF A PERSON.
There are many suggestions in the Gospels that Jesus ministered to a person's body, mind and spirit as a whole; that he had the gift of seeing people 'whole' – that he saw beyond a person's physical appearance, their reputation or their own estimate of themselves.

'Nathaniel asked him: "Where did you get to know me?"' (John 1:48)

'Which is easier, to say "Your sins are forgiven you" or to say "Stand up and walk"?' (Luke 5:23)

'"Come and see a man who told me everything I have ever done!"' (John 4:29)

'Then he said to her, "Your sins are forgiven ... your faith has saved you; go in peace."' (Luke 8:48–50)

'Then Jesus said to him, "Today salvation has come to this house ... for the Son of Man came to seek and to save the lost."' (Luke 19:9, 10)

'The woman came in fear and trembling ... He said to her, "Daughter, your faith has made you well; go in peace and be healed of your disease."' (Mark 5:33, 34)

'WHOLENESS' OR 'MATURITY' IS THE GOAL OF OUR LIVES.
Pastoral care therefore aims to help people on their way towards this goal. There are many ways of defining this 'maturity'.

St Paul speaks of people being 'conformed to the image of his Son' (Romans 8:29).

We observe that people do not stay the same, but are affected by many influences that cause them to change and grow. An important aid in seeing people 'whole' is to have an understanding of how human beings generally develop between birth and death; of how certain changes are caused and what they mean.

WE SEE A PERSON, NOT ONLY AS AN INDIVIDUAL, BUT ALSO AS PART OF A FAMILY AND COMMUNITY.

This has many implications for pastoral care.

- We don't do it on our own.
- The person we care for is not 'alone' – even if they live alone and/or feel alone.
- The care we give at the individual level is part of the transformation of society.
- We are working to make human institutions reflect 'Kingdom' values – 'to equip the saints for the work of ministry, for building up the body of Christ, until all of us come to the unity of the faith and of the knowledge of the Son of God, to maturity, to the measure of the full stature of Christ ... we must grow up in every way into him who is the head, into Christ, from whom the whole body, joined and knit together by every ligament with which it is equipped, as each part is working properly, promotes the body's growth in building itself up in love' (Ephesians 4:12–16).

WE SEE PEOPLE IN THE SETTING OF 'ETERNAL LIFE' AND ACCORDING TO VALUES THAT ARE NOT 'OF THIS WORLD'.

'Do not be conformed to this world, but be transformed by the renewing of your mind, so that you may discern what is the mind of God' (Romans 12:2).

For Session 4 BOUNDARIES

Informal pastoral care, unlike professional counselling, is not given at a set time or for an exact hour. People catch us unexpectedly: in the church porch, by the school gate or on the telephone just as we are sitting down to a meal. So those who want to be 'good neighbours', by responding to the needs of those around them, are often faced with difficulties in recognizing when these needs cannot – or should not – be met: in setting 'boundaries'. Friendly and supportive encounters can turn into emotional and persistent entanglements. The satisfaction of feeling we can help often blinds us to the necessity to let go or to suggest some other more appropriate source of care.

HOW MUCH TIME? WHEN SHOULD I SAY 'NO'?
When someone is in need of help the question soon arises: 'How much time can I give to supporting this person? How should I weigh this against the claims of the many other responsibilities in my life, including those of my family and of my own needs?' It is all too easy to take on too many responsibilities, leading eventually to feelings of being overloaded and overwhelmed – or even to serious stress. So in each situation we must give careful thought to whether our long-term involvement is appropriate, asking ourselves: 'Is it right that I should devote the time and energy to support a lone mother, parents at their wits' end or a man who has been made redundant? Am I the best person to help?' If the decision is 'no', it is important to convey this in a sensitive manner, so that the person does not feel snubbed or abandoned. We should suggest other resources or someone else who could help.

WHEN SHOULD I SAY 'YES'?
We may be faced with an urgent crisis and have no time to sit down and think. But even when we have been able to weigh up a situation with care, in the end we have to take a prayerful and intuitive decision. If Christian ministry is our response to God's

love, then it can never be guided by rational calculation alone. Sometimes we may have to dive in and take a risk for the Kingdom of God – shooting up 'arrow prayers' as we go – doing our best to act as we think Jesus would have done – even if it is not 'sensible'.

HOW CAN I BE INVOLVED BUT NOT OVERINVOLVED?

If we do take the step of offering 'care' to another person and get involved in visiting, chatting, listening and helping in practical ways, we need to give that person our full attention. But this does not mean that we have to give over our whole lives. We can mention other commitments and suggest time limits: 'Could you try to ring me before 6.00, as I have to prepare the evening meal then?' or, 'We can talk until it's time to fetch the children from school at 3.00', or, 'I shall be very busy for the next few days, so let's see how you are feeling after that...' We need to keep a certain distance if we are to be of any help, because we cannot listen effectively if we are overcome by sympathetic emotion.

There is a paradox here: one person cannot help another unless they genuinely 'care' and yet it is also true that they cannot help unless they can preserve some detachment. All of us who want to be 'good neighbours', including those whose work involves 'professional caring' (such as social workers, doctors or probation officers – and the clergy), need to practise a kind of 'loving detachment' if we are not to be overwhelmed.

HOW FAR SHOULD I TRY TO UNDERSTAND?

We should observe and respond to what is going on now rather than try to probe or delve into the past. We can make use of various 'tools for understanding', such as theories of human development and personality types, but they should be used to help us to empathize rather than to uncover. Although it is possible to draw close to another person, we must also accept that we are separate and different from each other and therefore the words 'I know how you feel' can never be true.

HOW CAN I AVOID KEEPING ANOTHER PERSON IN A STATE OF DEPENDENCE?

As a relationship develops it is helpful to get into the habit of observing our own motives and feelings. 'What am I gaining for myself and what will I lose when the giving of active and regular care is no longer necessary?' Through asking these questions we may see more clearly how to help other people to become increasingly self-assured and independent, rather than to boost our own self-esteem by keeping them dependent on us.

HOW CAN I BE CONFIDENT BUT NOT OVERCONFIDENT?

We need to believe that we can help in many situations. But we also need to be honest and humble enough to accept that we are not always the best person to help – and certainly not the only person who can help.

HOW CAN I DISTINGUISH BETWEEN AN 'EMERGENCY' NEED AND A LONG-TERM NEED?

Sometimes a person needs urgently to be listened to at a particular moment. We should not assume too readily that the person will continue needing a listener, but make it clear that such help is available if required. We could offer a phone number or say, 'You can always catch me after church on Sunday.'

WHAT IF I AM TORN IN TWO WAYS?

In a small community, especially for example in a rural area, people may be in both a 'neighbourly' and a 'professional' relationship with each other, which may raise problems about confidentiality and trust. Or you may be asked for help by people who are on opposite 'sides' in some complex local battle or by each of two people who are locked in a difficult relationship. In such situations it is always best to be open and avoid concealment. But it may be necessary to withdraw and hand over to someone who is not personally involved.

HOW CAN I CARE FOR SOMEONE WHO HAS DIFFERENT MORAL STANDARDS FROM ME, OR WHO I DISLIKE OR FIND IRRITATING?

Again it is always best to be open and ready to make our own views clear. But it is not necessary to thrust our views on to the other person. Our role is not to tell them what we think they should do, but to help them to sort our their problems for themselves.

Personal irritation is difficult to overcome, though it may be possible to hide it successfully. It may, however, be an indication that we should extricate ourselves from this relationship and help the person to find support elsewhere.

HOW CAN I TELL WHEN A PERSON NEEDS OTHER HELP?

We can develop a personal checklist of questions, to help us in deciding whether our involvement is appropriate:

- What is really happening here?
- What skills are needed to help in this situation? Do I have those skills?
- How much time and energy are likely to be needed? Would it be fair to myself or my family to commit myself to giving these regularly?
- If I get further into this, will it interfere with my relationship with this person in another setting – for example as patient/doctor or as a work colleague?
- Will this relationship upset someone else in this community? Does this matter?
- In this relationship will confidentiality be difficult to keep?
- Is help needed of a different kind from the help I can give?

More courses

There follow brief outlines of two courses for those who want to explore further. The sessions could be designed using similar plans and methods as in the Basic Course given in Chapter 11.

'Understanding and Caring'

A follow-on course of four sessions.

Aim
To enable those who join the course to explore how a better understanding of human personality can help them to care for their neighbours more effectively, by introducing some of the available 'tools for understanding' and by kindling awareness of the resources we all possess.

Session 1	'Listening to ourselves and to others'
Session 2	'How people develop'
Session 3	'Tools for understanding'
Session 4	'Some particular situations and issues'

'Taking a Lead'

A course of five sessions, each offering a biblical base, some theory and some practical exercises.

Aim
To enable those who exercise any kind of responsibility in a local church to develop leadership skills, by increasing their understanding of themselves, of how groups work and of how we communicate.

Session 1 What we mean by 'leadership'
- The distinguishing marks of Christian leadership
- Different styles of leadership
- Skills needed for leadership

Session 2 Relating to individuals
- Understanding human development, including faith development
- Looking at how the Church, in its life and worship – and especially through baptism and other 'rites of passage' – responds to the stages of human development

Session 3 Relating within a group
- How groups work
- Different kinds of group
- What makes an effective group

Session 4 Towards better meetings
- The skills needed for chairing or facilitating a meeting
- How to be a good committee member
- Resolving conflict and making decisions
- How to produce agendas and minutes

Session 5 Keeping the vision bright
- Communication
- Prayer

Evaluation – help for leaders to make future courses even more effective

At the end of a course valuable feedback can be elicited by asking each member to fill in an evaluation sheet. The most useful type encourages students to give time to producing thoughtful answers – rather than mere 'ticks in boxes'. But experience shows that it is difficult to persuade course members to go to the trouble of filling in such a questionnaire at home and then posting or delivering it to the course leader. Even when a stamped addressed envelope is provided, their consciences do not often prick them into action! So it is better to ask members to fill in a sheet at the close of the final session and give it in at once.

Three examples follow of questionnaires that have been used in recent years to evaluate 'Pastoral Care' courses. The first two have weaknesses: they illustrate the mistakes that can easily be made when one is devising such sheets. The third can be recommended.

Evaluation Sheet 1

(Note: this questionnaire takes some time to fill in adequately)

Please mark from 1 = very poor to 6 = very good. Give your reasons and any other comments you wish to add

VENUE – the Church Hall at Little Snoring.

CONTENT:
Session 1 'Better listening'

Session 2 'Why do we care?

Session 3 'Christian caring'

Session 4 'Looking forward'

TEACHING METHODS AND APPROACH
The teaching methods used

Talks/input

Homework

Discussion/group work

Hand-outs

Pastoral groups

Please answer as fully as you can — write on the back if you need to:

Would you like to have seen more or less emphasis placed on any particular areas?

Have you any comments on the tutor's style or competence?

Did you find any aspects of the course unhelpful?

Is there anything you would like to explore in another course?

How has the course helped you in developing your own ministry?

Any other comments?

Evaluation Sheet 2

(Note: this sheet would be difficult to use as it stands, because:
(a) Question 1 contains several questions, which would be clearer if separated.
(b) The wording of questions 2 and 3 seems to make unjustified assumptions.)

1   Did the course content give a good balance? Would you have preferred more or less emphasis placed on particular areas? Was there anything you would have liked to see covered by the course which was not included?

2   Were the teaching methods used appropriate and helpful?

3   What aspects of the course did you find particularly helpful in developing your own ministry?

4   Do you have any suggestions or comments which might help if a similar course is arranged in the future?

Evaluation Sheet 3

(Note: This could be done quite quickly, but also provides opportunities for more extended comment)

NAME (optional)

EVALUATION OF THE COURSE AS A WHOLE

Please score the course on the following grid:

0	25	50	75	100
very poor	poor	middling	good	very good

Give reasons for your score

What have been your major learnings from the course?

What has been most helpful about the course?

What has been least helpful about the course?

What was most helpful about the leader?

What was least helpful about the leader?

Some sample answers

'Ideas from others in the group were appreciated.'

'Huge topics that could have done with more time.'

'Glad to do a role play, even if finding it disconcerting.'

'Raised awareness of everyday applications.'

'Group work is still not my scene.'

'Helped me to get to know a small number of people better than otherwise.'

'Time will tell!'

'Great support that is continuing post course.'

'Made me realize how much caring and serving goes into a regular day. Stressed the importance of listening and silence. Now no longer afraid or ashamed to say when I can do nothing.'

'The course gave me confidence in my ability to offer pastoral care and increased my skills/tools.'

'I have gained a little more enlightenment, more awareness.'

'Increased knowledge. Encouragement to reflect on my experience. Issues raised that I had not previously thought about. Glad to experience different ways of learning.'

'Inspired to take it further and branch out by perhaps exploring further the counselling side. The group was very supportive.'

'Thank you for the careful, prayerful handling of the discussions; for the right atmosphere in which to enable a frank two-way flow of information and conversation.'

'A deeper insight into Christian caring and, as a result of it, knowing that Christian caring does exist in own parish.'

'Learned a lot about myself – more understanding.'

'The opportunity to compare experience with other committed people has been valuable. The leader gave a good input of information, but also respected the group's collective experience and enabled it to emerge. The course penetrated lots of "corners".'

EPILOGUE

A prayer for ending

Gracious and loving God,
thank you for bringing us together,
to think about how we can reflect your love more faithfully
in our caring for each other.
You have endowed us with varied gifts and responsibilities;
You challenge us to respond to your call.
Guide our uncertain steps;
Calm us when we are impatient;
Sustain us and help us to sustain each other;
that, through our listening, through our caring,
we may bring your love, your peace and your hope
to all your children.
Through Jesus, our Saviour and our Friend.

AMEN

NOTES

CT denotes the *Church Times*
CEN denotes the *Church of England Newspaper*

Chapter 1

1 Sally McFague, *Models of God*, Fortress Press, 1987
2 Alistair V. Campbell, *Rediscovering Pastoral Care*, DLT, 1981
3 Ibid. p. 37
4 Ibid. p. 59
5 Dr George Carey, *CEN*, October 1996
6 From the Mission Statement of an Anglican diocese
7 Janice Price, Secretary of the Church of England Board of Mission, *CEN*, 27 October 1996
8 Steve Rand, review of Tear Fund booklet *Mission and the Poor*, *CEN*, 1995
9 Canon Robert Warren, *Building Missionary Congregations*, Church House Publications, 1995, p. 3
10 Jackie Pullinger, newsletter from Hong Kong, 1995
11 David Deeks, *Pastoral Theology: An Enquiry*, Epworth Press, 1987, p. 80

12 Alistair V. Campbell, *Paid to Care?*, SPCK, 1985, p. 1
13 Jonathan Sacks, *The Times*, 24 February 1997

Chapter 2

1 Canon Tony Robinson describing ministry in an inner-city estate in Leicester, *CEN*, 24 March 1995
2 *CT*, 24 January 1997
3 *CEN*, 28 February 1997
4 *CT* and *CEN*, 31 January 1997
5 *CEN*, 6 December 1996
6 *Oxford Dictionary of Modern Quotations*, Oxford University Press, 1991, p. 66:3
7 *CEN*, 18 October 1996
8 Nancy Klein, *Women and Power*, BBC Books, 1993, p. 121
9 Kennedy and Charles, *On Becoming a Counsellor*, Gill and Macmillan Ltd, 1992, p. 57
10 *CT*, 8 December 1995
11 Howard Clinebell, *Basic Types of Pastoral Counselling*, Abingdon Press, 1966, p. 230
12 *CT*, 28 August 1996
13 Roger Hurding, *Roots and Shoots*, Hodder & Stoughton, 1985, p. 32

Chapter 3

1 Report on General Synod, *CEN*, 14 July 1996
2 Bishop David Sheppard, *CT* and *CEN*, 31 January 1997
3 Michael Bywater, *Independent on Sunday*, 6 August 1995
4 *CT*, 3 January 1997
5 *The Door* (Oxford Diocesan newspaper), February 1996
6 *Oxford Times*, 27 September 1996
7 *The Times*, 23 October 1996
8 *Guildford Diocesan Herald*, September 1996

9 From an essay by a mature student doing a 'Pastoral Care' course, 1995
10 Catriona Forbes, *Christian*, January 1961
11 Peter Crookes, *Country Way*, Summer 1996
12 Tessa Partridge, *The Door*, May 1996
13 CEN, 18 October 1996
14 The Times, 17 August 1994

Chapter 4

1 From a tribute to Bishop John Bone in *The Door*, November 1996
2 ADMINISTRY – 'We work with churches helping them to organise to evangelise ... we believe in good administration as a part of ministry ... good organisation is about people and their value, not paper and systems...' – PO Box 57, St Albans, AL1 3DT, Tel: 01727 856 370; Fax: 01727 843 765; E-mail: admini@ibm.net.

MODEM (Managerial and Organisational Disciplines for the Enhancement of Ministry) – 'exists to promote the relevance of sound management to the churches and the mutuality of interest between churches and secular organisations' – contact John Nelson on 01704 873973.

Chapter 5

1 Mark Birchall, *Modern Believing*, July 1994
2 Michael Hare-Duke, writing about recent developments in the Scottish Episcopal Church, *CT*, 1994
3 Rover Group, *Total Quality Handbook*, 1995
4 L.C. Bridges, in a private letter
5 *The Times*, 27 March 1995
6 Rover Group, *Total Quality Handbook*, 1995

7 *The Times*, 24 February 1996
8 The Rev. Keith Lamdin, Director of Training for Oxford Diocese, *The Door*, June 1996

Chapter 6

1 *CT*, 16 September 1994
2 *CT*, 30 September 1994
3 Walter Raleigh, 'The Author's Epitaph, Made by Himself', written the night before his death.

Chapter 7

1 Letter in *The Times*, 29 January 1996
2 *The Times*, 7 November 1996
3 Cardinal Basil Hume, *The Tablet*, January 1996
4 Letter from a lay organizer of marriage preparation courses, *CEN*, 8 April 1994
5 William Shakespeare, sonnet no. 116

Chapter 8

1 From a baptism sermon by Rev. Chris Mackenna, *The Times*, 11 November 1996
2 John Nelson (ed.), *Management and Ministry*, Canterbury Press 1996, chapter 6
3 Attractive baptism cards (with designs that came originally from Norway) are produced by the Mothers' Union in the Diocese of Carlisle.
4 Rev. Robbie Lowe, *Directions*, February 1997

Chapter 9

1 Betty Pulkingham, quoted in CPAS Magazine, Spring 1996
2 Report by the Church of Scotland's Panel on Worship, *CT*, 15 April 1994
3 Most Rev. Winston Ndungane, Archbishop of Cape Town, *CT*, 27 September 1996
4 Monica Furlong, *Bird of Paradise: Glimpses of a Living Myth*, Mowbray, 1995, p. 24
5 Evelyn Underhill, *Worship*, James Nisbet & Co. Ltd, 1936
6 *CEN*, October 1995
7 *CEN*, 26 January 1996
8 Evelyn Waugh, *Diary*, entry for 3 January 1954, Weidenfeld & Nicolson, 1976
9 *CEN*, 10 February 1995
10 Most Rev. Winston Ndungane, *CT*, September 1996
11 Church of England, *Alternative Service Book*, Rite A, Post-Communion prayer
12 Quoted in a University Sermon in Oxford, 1992
13 Bishop Michael Marshall, *CEN*, September 1994
14 Church of England, *Alternative Service Book*, Rite A
15 *CEN*, 17 January 1997
16 Ronald Blythe, *CT*, 25 April 1997
17 F. Pratt Green, *Hymns Ancient & Modern New Standard*, No. 464.

Chapter 10

1 Quoted in a church magazine, original source unknown.
2 Dr George Carey, New Year Address, *The Times*, 1 January 1997
3 Stephen Parsons, *Searching for Healing*, Lion, 1995
4 Stephen Parsons, *The Challenge of Christian Healing*, SPCK, 1986

5 Morris Maddocks, *The Christian Healing Ministry*, SPCK, 1981
6 Canon Gordon Jeff, *CT*, 26 April 1996

Chapter 11

1 For example:

Scripture Union, 207-209 Queensway, Bletchley, Milton Keynes, MK2 2EB
Upside Down Trust (formerly Training and Development Unit) 26–36 Heathcoat Street, Nottingham, NG1 3AA
CPAS, Athena Drive, Tachbrook Park, Warwick, CV34 6NG

Chapter 12

1 Alistair Campbell, *Rediscovering Pastoral Care*, DLT, 1981, chapters 3–5